essential Origami

essential Origami

Paul Jackson

HH
HERMES HOUSE

PUBLISHER'S NOTE

No occupation is gentler than papercraft, but some general points
should be remembered for safety and care of the environment.

▮ Always choose non-toxic materials whenever possible; for example
PVA, strong clear glue, non-toxic varnishes and poster paints.

▮ Craft knives, scissors and all cutting implements should be used
with care. Children love papercrafts, but should only be
allowed to use sharp tools under supervision.

▮ Always use a cutting board or cutting mat to avoid
damage to household surfaces (it is also safer to
cut onto a firm, hard surface).

▮ Protect surfaces from paint, glue and varnish splashes by
laying down old newspapers.

This edition published in 1998 by Hermes House

© Anness Publishing Limited 1995

Hermes House is an imprint of Anness Publishing Limited
Hermes House, 88-89 Blackfriars Road
London SE1 8HA

ISBN 1 84038 114 0

A CIP catalogue record for this book
is available from the British Library

Printed and bound in Singapore

1 3 5 7 9 10 8 6 4 2

CONTENTS

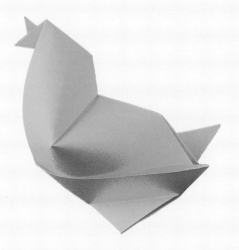

∎ INTRODUCTION

It is not difficult to understand why origami is the most popular of all papercrafts: the art is very inexpensive, can be done anywhere at anytime and requires no equipment or facilities other than a sheet of paper and a firm surface to work on. Moreover, the transformation of an ordinary piece of paper into a pleasing origami design is a kind of alchemy, perhaps even more so in today's increasingly push-button, computer-controlled, battery-operated culture, than ever before.

The history of origami is rather obscure, but clearly cannot pre-date the invention of paper in China about two thousand years ago. The word 'origami' is not Chinese but Japanese, and is used worldwide out of respect for the ancestral home of the art. When China invaded Japan in AD 610, the secret of papermaking travelled with them and was immediately assimilated into Japanese culture, not just as origami, but more practically as screens, mats, bags, umbrellas, woven clothes and many other objects. As an indication of the importance of paper to the Japanese, the word 'origami' is formed from 'ori' (to fold) and 'kami'

meaning paper and also God ('kami' becomes 'gami' when combined with 'ori'). Indeed, many of the early origami designs were created for symbolic or ceremonial purposes, not for recreation.

The growth of creative origami in the West began in the 1950s, though it was a minor Spanish tradition and practised by the occasional creative individual before that time. Curiously, since that same decade, the art has also undergone a major creative revival in Japan, so much so that there are now several hundred Japanese language books currently in print, most containing new creative work. A great amount of new work is also coming from the West, in all manner of styles ranging from the charmingly simple to the astonishingly complex and from the expressive to the geometric.

If you are new to origami the next few pages will introduce the basics. Readers who have folded before will find these pages a useful refresher. The designs which follow have been graded according to their level of difficulty and you are encouraged not to be too ambitious too soon.

ORIGAMI PAPER

Although origami is defined as 'the art of *paper* folding', most paper folders spend little time thinking about paper, preferring to get straight down to the business of folding, frequently with whatever paper happens to be to hand, however inappropriate it may be. A little consideration for paper, though, can significantly improve the look of what you make and increase your pleasure in folding it.

The easiest and cheapest source of good quality practice paper is photocopy (Xerox) paper. The photocopy and quick print shops now found in most shopping centres sell reams (packets of 500 sheets) of white or coloured photocopy paper, either A4 size or American Letter Size (both about the same size as a page in this book). The shop will trim a ream to square on a power guillotine for a nominal sum. Two or three reams can usually be purchased for a very reasonable price. Part-reams may also be purchased.

For two-tone models, origami paper bought in packets is ideal. However, it can be difficult to find and is relatively expensive. Also, the bright colours can make some designs look rather childish, so it should be used with care. Patterned gift-wrap paper is a good alternative if origami paper cannot be found. Other good practice papers include computer paper, typing paper, writing paper and even brown wrapping paper.

For displaying origami, perhaps at home or at a place of work, quality papers appropriate to the design should be used. A surprising range of interesting papers can be found in art, craft and graphic equipment supplies shops. It is also worth starting a collection of unusual papers such as old posters, discarded wrapping paper, wallpaper and telephone note blocks.

TIPS

In many ways, nothing could be more basic than folding a sheet of paper. Yet, despite this wonderful simplicity, there are a few guidelines to follow that will make the process of folding easier and very satisfying. Please follow them.

- Check that the paper you are folding is *exactly* square. The best method for making a square is described in the following pages. Nothing is more frustrating than trying to fold paper which is not quite square!

- Do not fold against a soft surface, such as a carpet, your lap or bedsheets. Fold against a hard surface such as a large hardback book or a table.

- Crease slowly, firmly and accurately. Form the early creases with particular care – if they are incorrectly placed, all the later, smaller creases will be difficult to place accurately and will look messy.

- Read the instructions and follow the symbols on each step. Many a mistake is made by ignoring written instructions or by not following all the written instructions on a step, particularly during complex manoeuvres.

- The instructions and symbols on one step will create a shape which looks like the next step but stripped of its symbols. So, you must always *look ahead* to the next step to see what shape you are trying to make. Never look at steps in isolation, but see them as being interconnected, like links in a chain.

ORIGAMI SOCIETIES

If you would like to know more about origami, here are addresses for two well-organized societies. Both accept overseas members and welcome beginners. Also, both publish regular magazines, hold conventions and regional meetings, sell a wide variety of books and paper, and publish booklets on specialist origami topics. The British Origami Society has a postal library service.

British Origami Society,
253 Park Lane,
Poynton,
Stockport,
Cheshire,
SK12 1RH,
England.

The Friends of the Origami Centre of America,
15 West 77th Street,
New York,
NY 10024,
USA.

The Japanese Paper Place,
966 Queen Street West,
Toronto M6J 1G8,
Canada.

The Australian Origami Society,
2/5 Broome Street,
Highgate,
Perth 6000,
Australia.

The New Zealand Origami Society,
79 Dunbar Road,
Christchurch 3,
New Zealand.

Most papers are bought as rectangular sheets that need to be trimmed square before being folded. Here, then, is a quick and simple way to accurately trim a large sheet to a smaller square, ensuring that the edges are kept straight and clean.

1 Fold over an edge of the sheet, lining up the edges at the sides to ensure square corners.

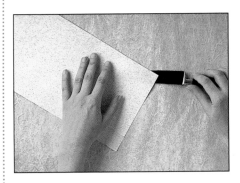

2 Carefully cut along the crease with a series of large, smooth slicing movements, made with a non-serrated kitchen knife (one with a 15 cm [6 in] blade is best). Set aside the unwanted portion of the sheet.

3 Fold over the short edge to make a triangle.

4 Bend the sheet backwards and make a crease underneath the bottom edge of the triangle.

5 Cut along the crease.

6 Unfold the triangle.

7 The square complete.

OTHER METHODS

Scissors
Duplicate the method shown in the photographs, but use scissors instead of a non-serrated knife. Be careful to control the cutting to ensure a straight edge.

Craft knife
Duplicate the method shown in the photographs, but unfold each crease and cut along them with a craft knife held against a metal rule. Before cutting, place thick card beneath the paper so that the knife does not damage your work surface.

Guillotine
Paper bought in bulk from photocopy print shops and cut on the premises on a power guillotine will be perfectly square, but paper cut by hand on a manually-operated guillotine has the annoying habit of never quite being square, whatever safeguards are taken. So, hand guillotining is not recommended if it is important that your paper is perfectly proportioned.

Tearing
Tearing is not recommended, but is acceptable if there is no other way to trim paper. Before tearing, crease the folded edge backwards and forwards several times, pressing firmly. This will weaken the crease and make tearing easier and neater.

■ S Y M B O L S

No sequence of origami diagrams can be followed without an understanding of the symbols they use. The meaning of most symbols is obvious and it is not necessary to learn them all now, but it would be very helpful to at least learn the difference between the mountain and valley fold symbols. The other symbols can be learnt as they appear by referring back to this page.

The same symbols can be found in most origami books, whatever language they are written in, be it English, Spanish or even Japanese. This standardization means that the language of origami is truly universal, and that enthusiasts can fold from almost any book, East or West.

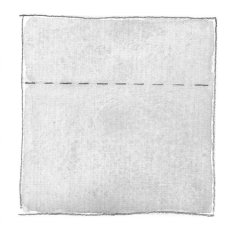

■ valley

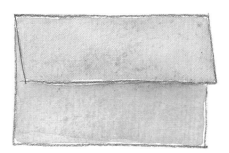

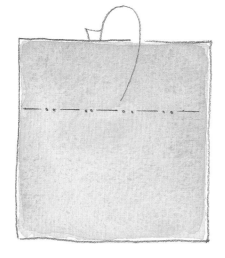

■ mountain

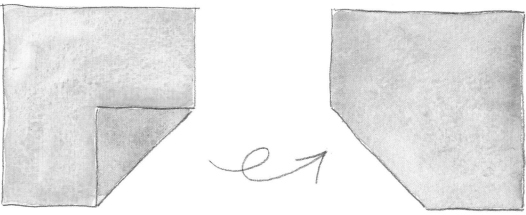

■ existing creases

■ turn over

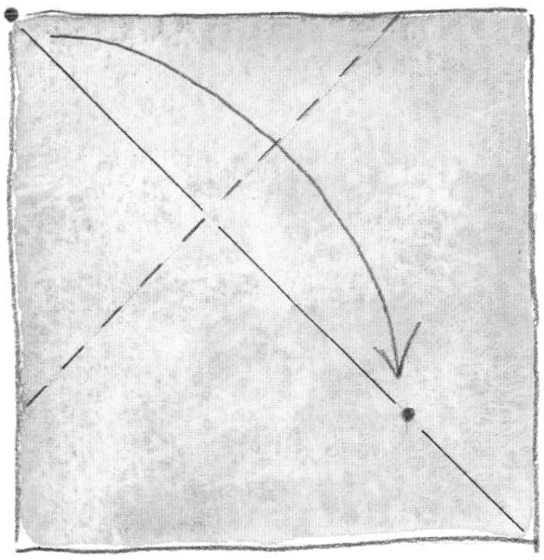

■ fold dot to dot

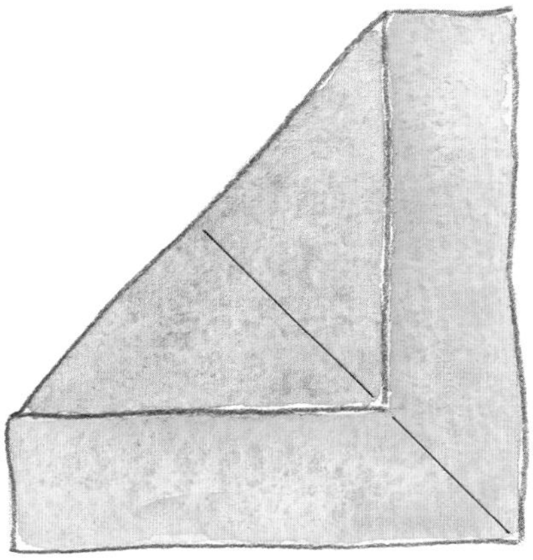

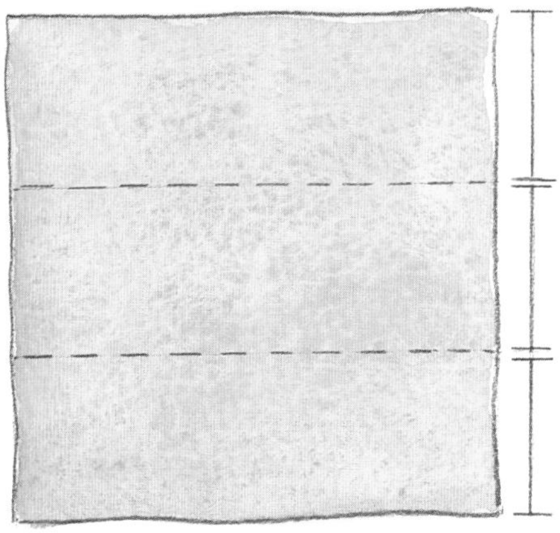

■ these distances are
   equal

■ unfold or pull out

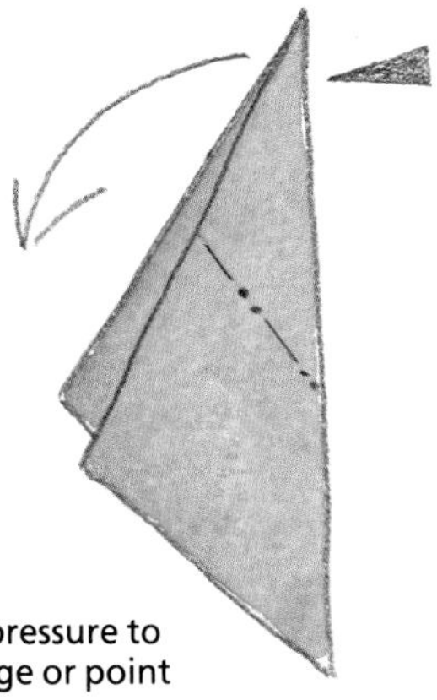

■ apply pressure to
   this edge or point

■ inflate

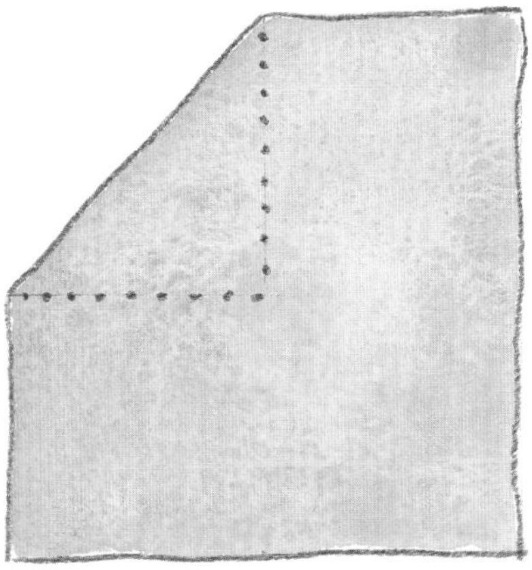

■ x-ray view

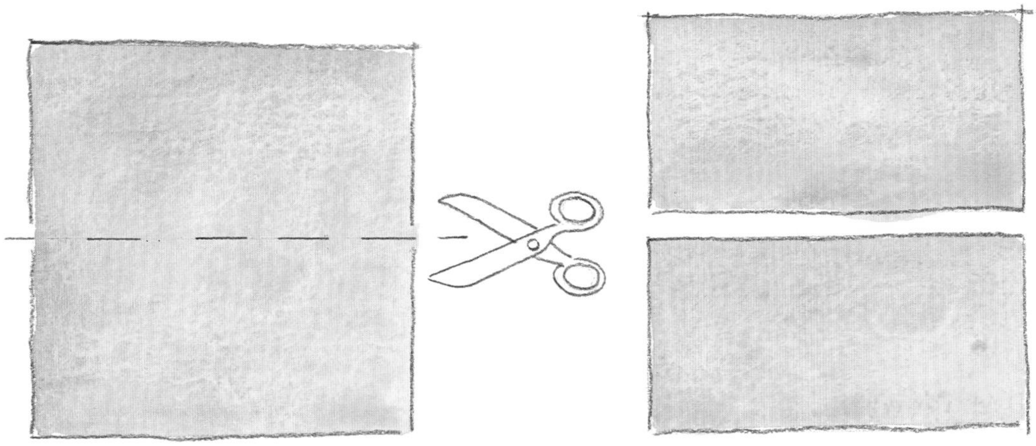

■ cut

Apart from the basic mountain and valley creases from which all origami designs are folded, there are four advanced techniques found in the designs that follow. These techniques are used in combination and are: the squash fold, the sink fold and the inside and outside reverse folds. However, not all designs use these advanced techniques, and only the Elephant uses them all together.

Squash and sink folds are the least common. To save space, a detailed explanation of each is given once in the book within a particular design. For an explanation of the squash fold see the Multiform House, Steps 4–6 for an explanation of the sink fold see the Star, Steps 8–12. When you come across a squash or sink fold in another design, refer to these designs for a step-by-step guide.

Inside and outside reverse folds are not more complex than squash or sink folds, but are more common and come in a greater variety. So, to simplify cross referencing, here are the basic forms of each. Refer to this page whenever you need to be reminded how to make them.

INSIDE REVERSE

Pull-through version

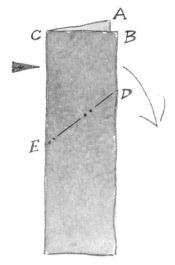

1 This is how the manoeuvre is illustrated in the book.

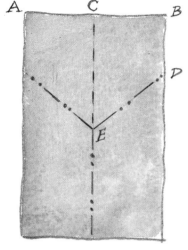

2 This is the crease pattern.

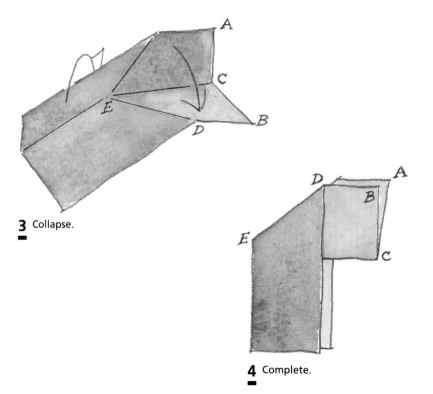

3 Collapse.

4 Complete.

Push-in version

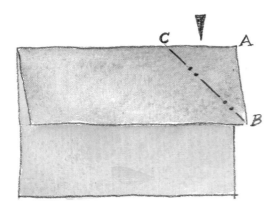

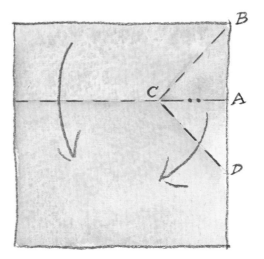

1 This is how the manoeuvre is illustrated in the book.

2 This is the crease pattern.

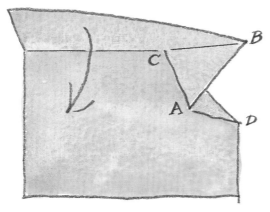

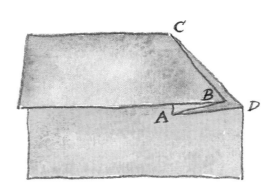

3 Collapse.

4 Complete.

OUTSIDE REVERSE

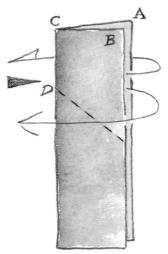

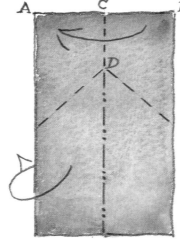

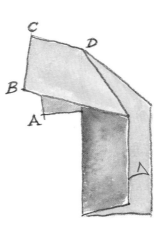

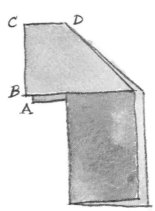

1 This is how the manoeuvre is illustrated in the book.

2 This is the crease pattern.

3 Collapse.

4 Complete.

SIMPLE PROJECTS

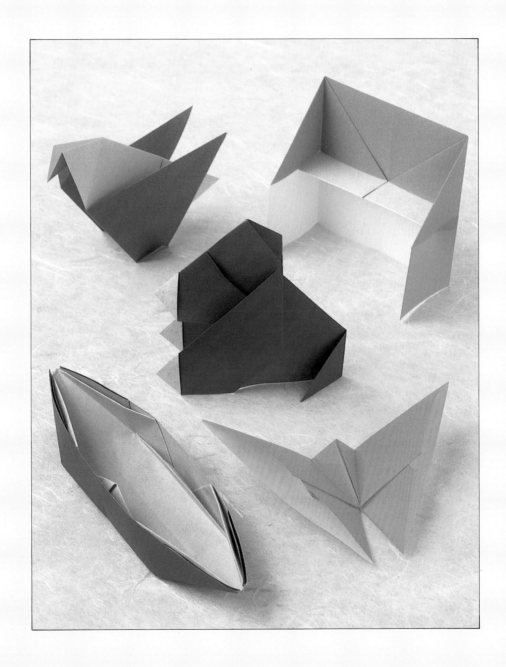

GLIDER

This design is one of a number of similar gliders of Chinese origin, all of which fly extremely well. The secret of good paper plane making is to fold with great accuracy and to practise a variety of launching actions – a carefully-made plane will not fly well if launched wrongly. Use an A4 or American Letter Size sheet of paper.

Traditional design.

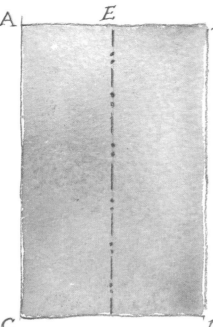

1 Fold the sheet in half down the middle, as a mountain fold (it is easier to make a valley fold, then to turn the sheet over). Unfold.

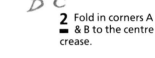

2 Fold in corners A & B to the centre crease.

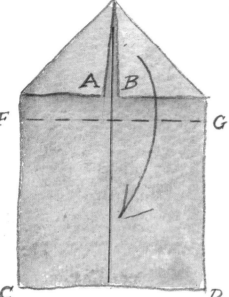

3 Fold down E along crease FG. Note that FG is a little below the level of AB.

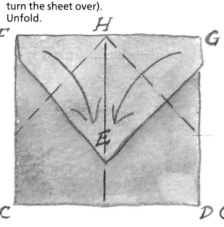

4 Fold in corners F & G, leaving E exposed.

5 Fold up E over F & G.

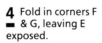

6 Mountain fold D to C.

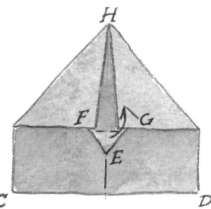

7 Before creasing, press flat the existing creases. Then, make the wing creases from the nose tip at H.

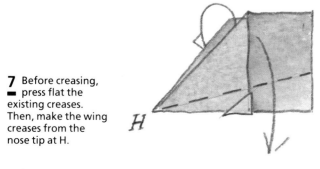

8 The Glider complete. Hold as shown at the point of balance, the wings forming a slight 'V' shape. Release smoothly but firmly.

■ C A N D Y B A G

If folded from greaseproof paper, this practical design will hold fries and other oily or sticky foods. For extra strength, fold two squares together. For sweets or candies, use any paper, not too thin. Use a 15–25 cm (6–10 in) square. If using origami paper, start coloured side up.

Designed by Paul Jackson.

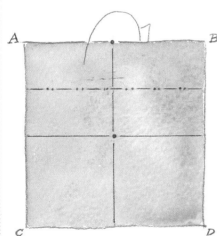

1 Fold and unfold the paper in half horizontally and vertically. Mountain fold edge AB to the centre crease.

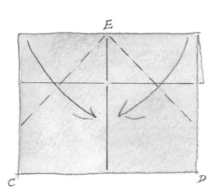

2 Fold in the top corners to the centre crease.

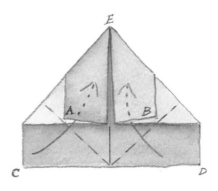

3 Similarly, fold in bottom corners C & D, but tucking them beneath A & B, to lock them flat.

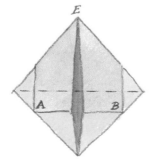

4 Valley fold in half across the middle, then . . .

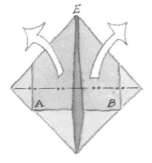

5 . . . mountain fold in half, to create a flexible crease. Open out the bag.

6 The Candy Bag complete.

BUTTERFLY

There are a great many origami butterflies in all manner of styles, some very complex. This is one of the simplest. It is important to use origami paper, so that white triangles appear at the edges between the coloured wings, to visually separate them. Cut a square of origami paper in half to create a 2 × 1 rectangle. Start coloured side up.

Designed by Paul Jackson.

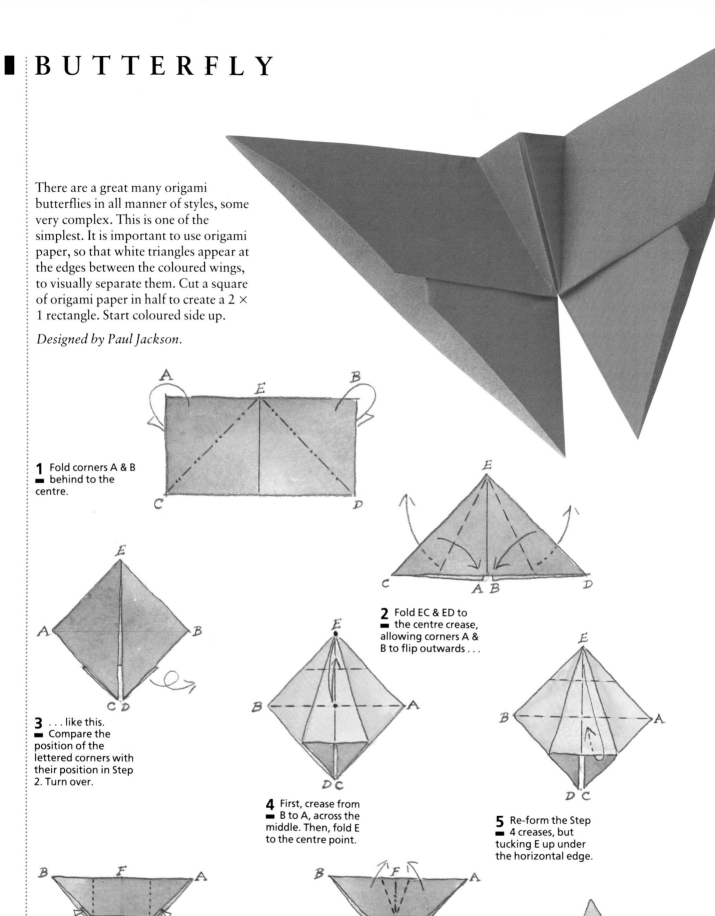

1 Fold corners A & B behind to the centre.

2 Fold EC & ED to the centre crease, allowing corners A & B to flip outwards . . .

3 . . . like this. Compare the position of the lettered corners with their position in Step 2. Turn over.

4 First, crease from B to A, across the middle. Then, fold E to the centre point.

5 Re-form the Step 4 creases, but tucking E up under the horizontal edge.

6 With vertical creases that run inside up to edge BA, mountain fold the loose corners behind as far as they will go.

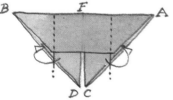

7 Make a mountain and two valley creases where shown, to create the body and to swivel D & C apart.

8 The Butterfly complete.

■ S A M P A N

This is a simplified version of a sampan
with a canopy over each end of the
boat. Both designs feature an
extraordinary move, here shown in
Steps 7–9, in which the entire shape is
turned inside out. With a little extra
folding, one end of the sampan can be
blunted to create a rowing boat. Use a
square of paper. If using origami paper,
start coloured side up.

Traditional design.

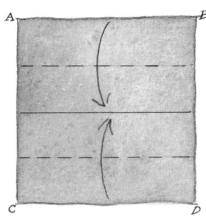

1 Crease and
■ unfold across the
centre. Fold the top
and bottom edges to
the crease.

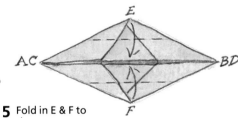

2 Fold in the
■ corners.

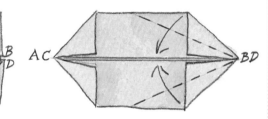

3 Narrow the
■ corner at the
right, as though
making the familiar
paper dart.

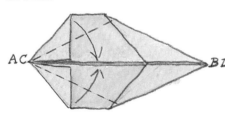

4 Repeat at the left,
■ overlapping the
Step 4 creases.

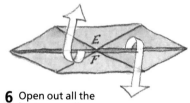

5 Fold in E & F to
■ the centre crease.
The paper is thick, so
press firmly.

6 Open out all the
■ layers revealing
the coloured base
. . .

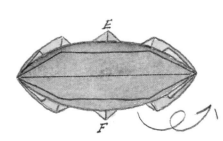

7 . . . like this, to
■ form a loose boat
shape. Turn over.

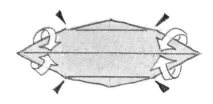

8 To lock the
■ sampan, push
down on the four
arrowed corners, so
that the whole of
the structure inverts
and turns inside out!

9 The Sampan
■ complete.

N A P K I N F O L D S

Napkin folds always create a point of interest on a dining table. The Duck Step is a basic form from which other varieties of napkin fold can be made. The Cable Buffet server allows guests at a buffet or picnic to help themselves to food, a napkin and cutlery all at once, while the Bishop's elegant curves and free-standing structure create a strong impact on any table.

Designed by Paul Jackson.

D U C K S T E P

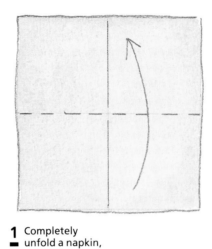

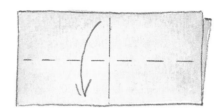

2 Fold the top edge down to the crease.

1 Completely unfold a napkin, then fold the bottom edge up to the top.

3 Fold each half of the top edge down the centre crease . . .

4 . . . like this. Turn the napkin over.

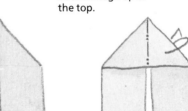

5 Mountain fold the right side behind the left.

6 Valley fold the front square up over the triangle. Repeat behind.

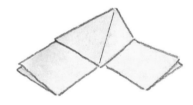

7 The Duck Step napkin complete.

CABLE BUFFET

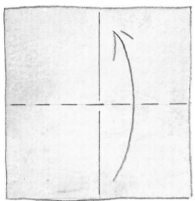

1 Completely unfold a napkin, then fold the bottom edge up to the top.

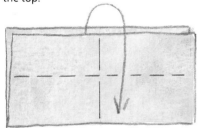

2 Fold the top layer down to the crease.

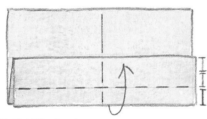

3 Fold the top layer back up a little way . . .

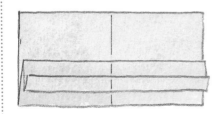

4 . . . like this. Turn the napkin over.

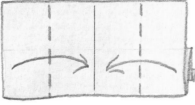

5 Fold the sides to the middle.

6 Tuck one half deep into the other, locking the napkin flat.

7 The Cable Buffet server complete. Insert cutlery into the pocket ready for the meal.

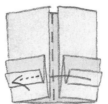

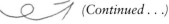

(Continued . . .)

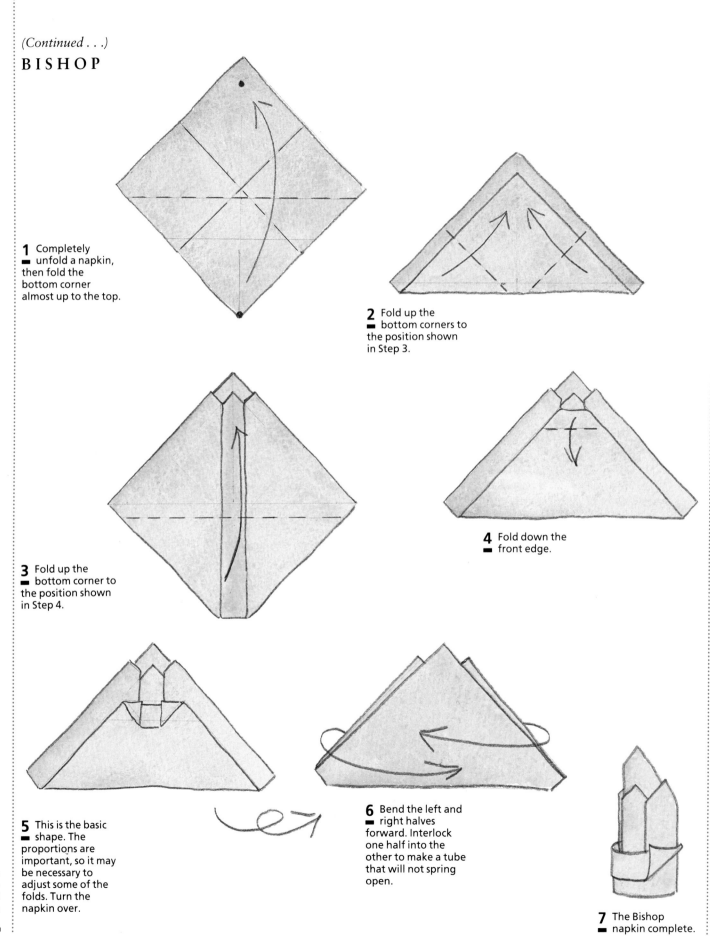

(Continued . . .)

BISHOP

1 Completely unfold a napkin, then fold the bottom corner almost up to the top.

2 Fold up the bottom corners to the position shown in Step 3.

3 Fold up the bottom corner to the position shown in Step 4.

4 Fold down the front edge.

5 This is the basic shape. The proportions are important, so it may be necessary to adjust some of the folds. Turn the napkin over.

6 Bend the left and right halves forward. Interlock one half into the other to make a tube that will not spring open.

7 The Bishop napkin complete.

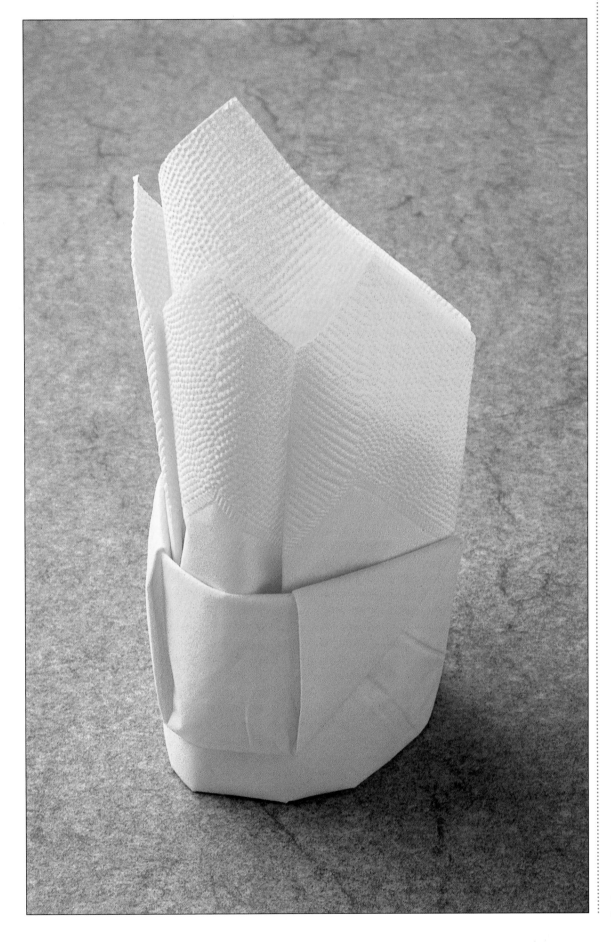

FISH

The creator of this fish is known for designs which are pre-creased and collapsed into shape. When pre-creasing, it is important to fold accurately (here, up to Step 5), otherwise the creases will not fall into place to achieve Step 6. For extra flatness, a speck of glue inside the mouth will close the layers. Use a square of origami paper, coloured side up, or a square with the same colour on both sides.

Designed by Jeff Beynon, UK.

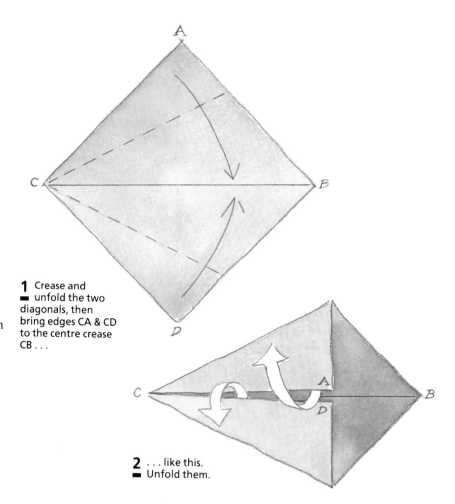

1 Crease and unfold the two diagonals, then bring edges CA & CD to the centre crease CB . . .

2 . . . like this. Unfold them.

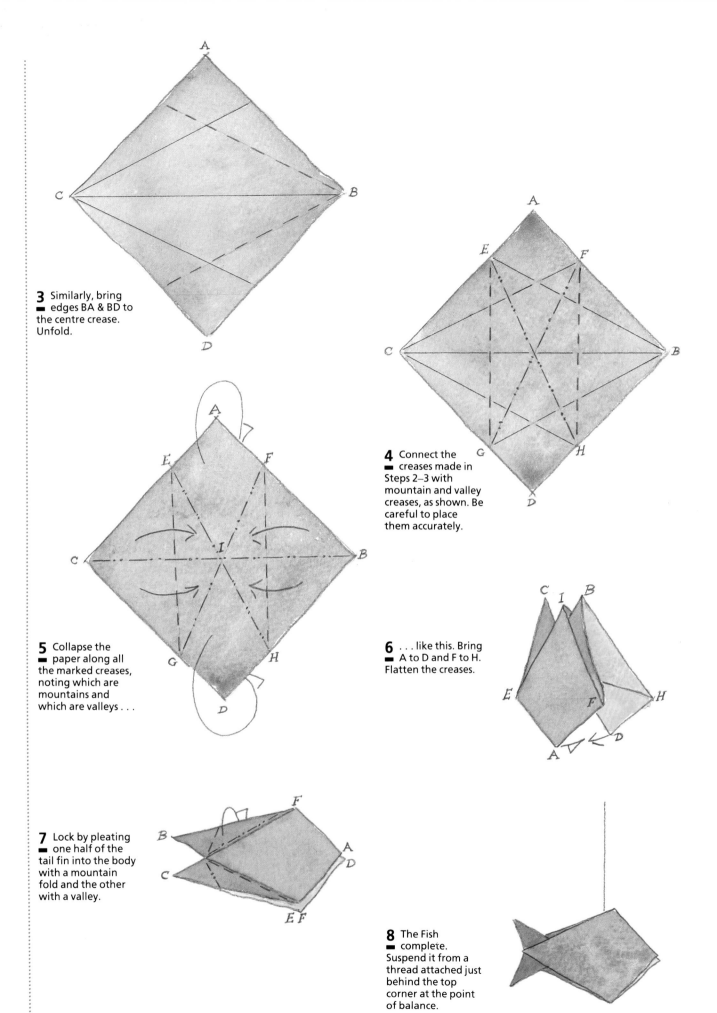

3 Similarly, bring
edges BA & BD to
the centre crease.
Unfold.

4 Connect the
creases made in
Steps 2–3 with
mountain and valley
creases, as shown. Be
careful to place
them accurately.

5 Collapse the
paper along all
the marked creases,
noting which are
mountains and
which are valleys . . .

6 . . . like this. Bring
A to D and F to H.
Flatten the creases.

7 Lock by pleating
one half of the
tail fin into the body
with a mountain
fold and the other
with a valley.

8 The Fish
complete.
Suspend it from a
thread attached just
behind the top
corner at the point
of balance.

SLEEPY DOG

The design is simple to make, but it is important to place C accurately in Steps 1 & 2. Once Step 3 has been achieved, the remaining folds fall naturally into place. Note the way in which the eyes are suggested. Use a square of origami paper, coloured side up.

Designed by Paul Jackson.

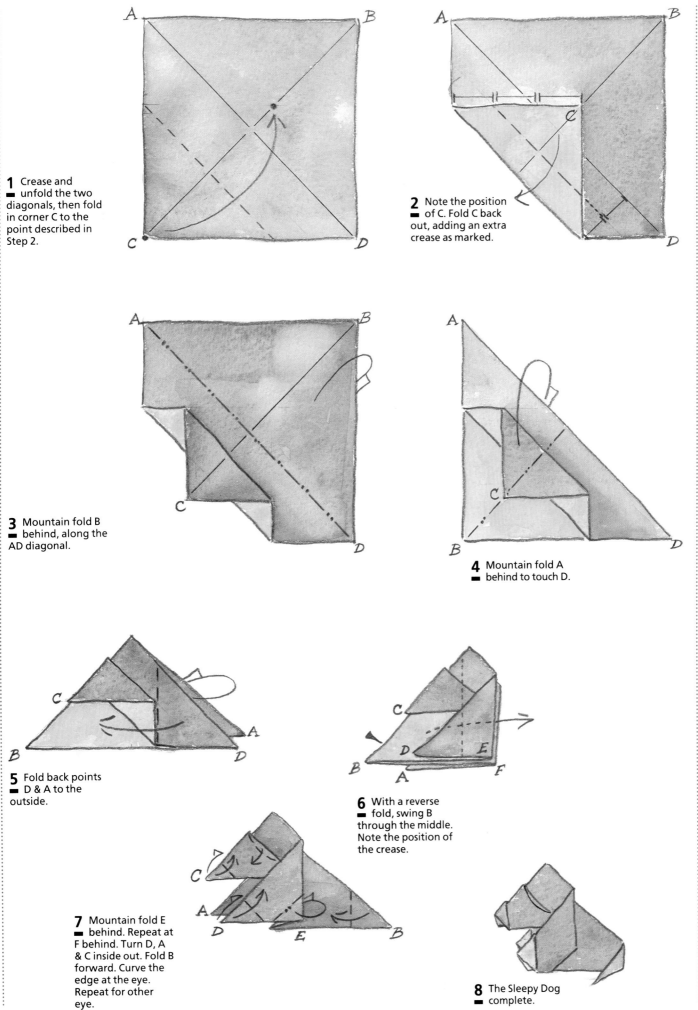

1 Crease and unfold the two diagonals, then fold in corner C to the point described in Step 2.

2 Note the position of C. Fold C back out, adding an extra crease as marked.

3 Mountain fold B behind, along the AD diagonal.

4 Mountain fold A behind to touch D.

5 Fold back points D & A to the outside.

6 With a reverse fold, swing B through the middle. Note the position of the crease.

7 Mountain fold E behind. Repeat at F behind. Turn D, A & C inside out. Fold B forward. Curve the edge at the eye. Repeat for other eye.

8 The Sleepy Dog complete.

MODULAR DECORATION I

A modular design is one in which a number of identical units are folded, then locked together without glue to create a decoration or geometric form. Other modular designs are included and appear later. In recent years, it has become a very popular branch of origami, East and West. Method 1 begins with a rectangle, Method 2 with a small square.

Designed by Paul Jackson.

METHOD 1

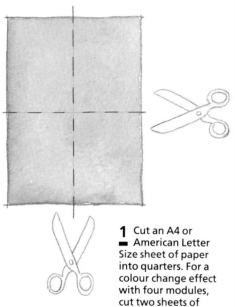

1 Cut an A4 or American Letter Size sheet of paper into quarters. For a colour change effect with four modules, cut two sheets of different colours.

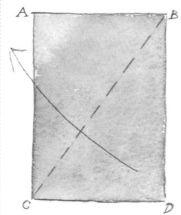

2 Take one quarter sheet of paper and fold diagonal BC.

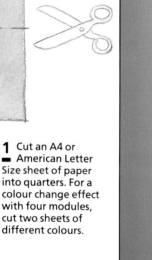

3 Fold A behind and D to the front.

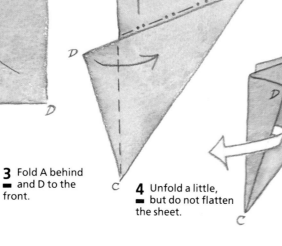

4 Unfold a little, but do not flatten the sheet.

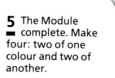

5 The Module complete. Make four: two of one colour and two of another.

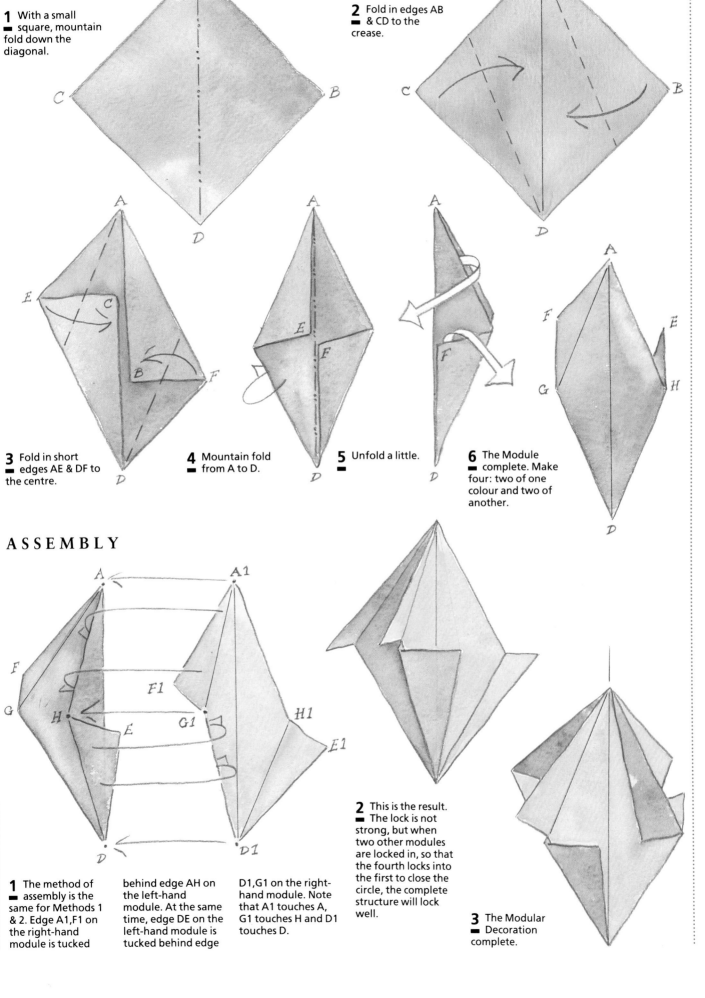

METHOD 2

1 With a small square, mountain fold down the diagonal.

2 Fold in edges AB & CD to the crease.

3 Fold in short edges AE & DF to the centre.

4 Mountain fold from A to D.

5 Unfold a little.

6 The Module complete. Make four: two of one colour and two of another.

ASSEMBLY

1 The method of assembly is the same for Methods 1 & 2. Edge A1,F1 on the right-hand module is tucked behind edge AH on the left-hand module. At the same time, edge DE on the left-hand module is tucked behind edge D1,G1 on the right-hand module. Note that A1 touches A, G1 touches H and D1 touches D.

2 This is the result. The lock is not strong, but when two other modules are locked in, so that the fourth locks into the first to close the circle, the complete structure will lock well.

3 The Modular Decoration complete.

COLOUR-CHANGE BIRD

This design is included because it is a
particular favourite. The simple shape
of the completed bird and the
effectiveness of the colour contrasts are
achieved by a fluent and concise
sequence of folds. Perhaps it is too
stylized for some readers, but less can
sometimes be more. Use a square of
origami paper, white side up.

Designed by Paul Jackson.

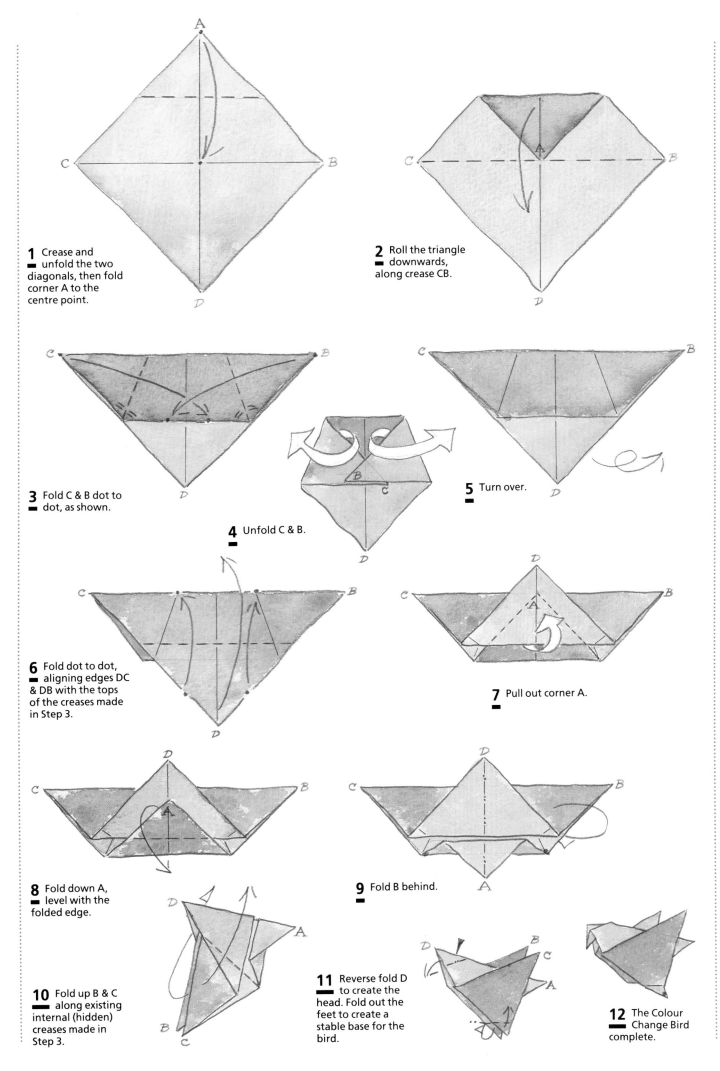

1 Crease and unfold the two diagonals, then fold corner A to the centre point.

2 Roll the triangle downwards, along crease CB.

3 Fold C & B dot to dot, as shown.

4 Unfold C & B.

5 Turn over.

6 Fold dot to dot, aligning edges DC & DB with the tops of the creases made in Step 3.

7 Pull out corner A.

8 Fold down A, level with the folded edge.

9 Fold B behind.

10 Fold up B & C along existing internal (hidden) creases made in Step 3.

11 Reverse fold D to create the head. Fold out the feet to create a stable base for the bird.

12 The Colour Change Bird complete.

MODULAR DECORATION II

The basic modules are very simple to make, but some thought must be given to assembling them correctly. Once locked, they will hold together very well. For re-use – perhaps from one Christmas to the next – the decoration may be flattened for easy storage. Use two 10–15 cm (4–6 in) squares of paper. If using origami paper, start with the white side up.

Designed by Paul Jackson.

METHOD

1 Crease and fold a vertical diagonal, then fold D up to A.

2 Fold edge AD,B forward to the vertical crease (valley fold) and edge AD,C behind to that crease (mountain fold).

3 This is the completed module. Make another.

ASSEMBLY

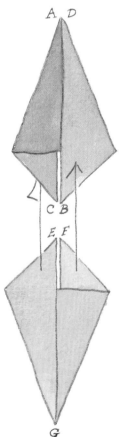

1 Take careful note of the lettered corners. Bring the two modules together, so that F is on top of B, and C is on top of E . . .

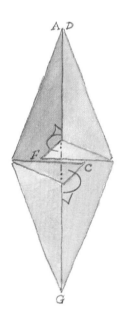

2 . . . like this. Fold F across to the horizontal. Repeat with C, then with E & B behind.

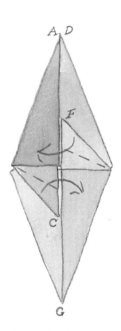

3 Lock the modules together by tucking F & C behind the vertical edges. Repeat behind with E & B.

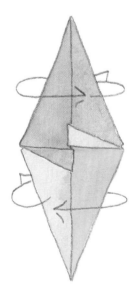

4 Separate the modules by twisting one away from the other, so that they lie perpendicular to each other.

5 The Modular Decoration complete. Suspend from a thread.

Here is a remarkable sequence of designs which are all made from the same basic shape, the House. The designs shown here are not the full set: it is also possible to fold a dustpan, purse, fox puppet, crown . . . and very probably many others! Experiment by folding the paper this way and that to see what you can discover. Use a square of origami paper, white side up.

Traditional design.

HOUSE

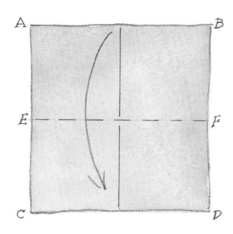

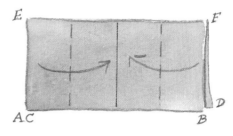

1 Crease and unfold down the middle of a square, then fold AB down to CD.

2 Fold the edges to the centre.

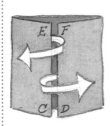

3 Unfold.

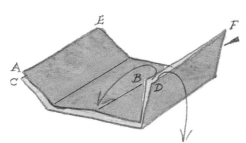

4 Lift up the edge BD,F. Separate B from D, applying pressure on the edges below F . . .

5 . . . like this. Pull B & D right apart and squash F flat.

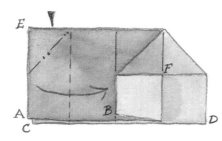

6 Repeat Steps 4–5 on the left, separating A from C and squashing E flat. Let A touch B.

7 The House complete. Children like to draw windows and a door to finish the design.

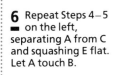

3D HOUSE

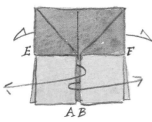

1 Begin with Step 6 of the House. Fold C & D behind.

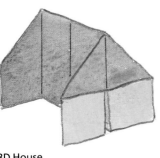

2 Unfold AC & BD.

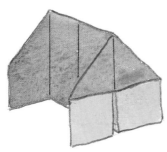

3 The 3D House complete.

(Continued . . .)

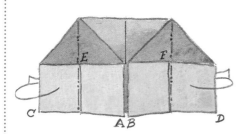

SEAT

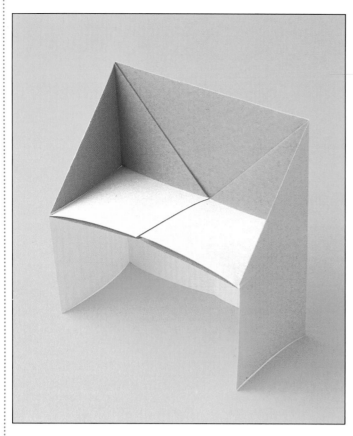

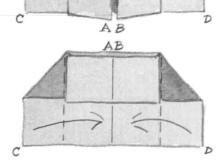

1 Begin with Step 6 of the House. Fold AB up to the top edge.

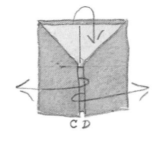

2 Fold in C & D.

3 Swing open C & D and pull down AB.

4 The Seat complete.

ORGAN

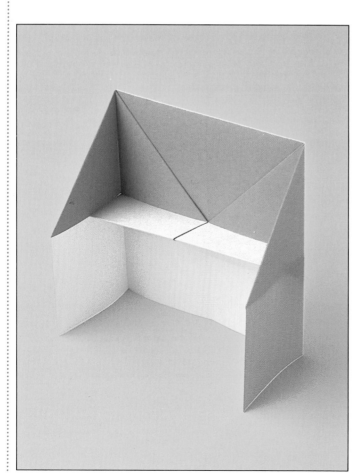

1 Begin with Step 2 of the Seat. Fold edge AB back down to the folded edge across the middle of the paper.

2 Fold in C & D.

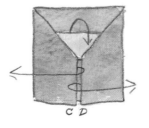

3 Swing open C & D and pull down the ledge.

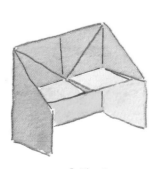

4 The Organ complete.

G.I. CAP

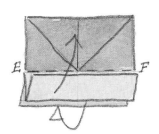

1 Begin with Step 2 ■ of the 3D House. Fold AB up to EF. Repeat behind.

2 Fold up the ■ bottom section along crease EF. Repeat behind.

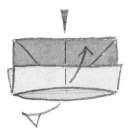

3 Open out the cap. ■

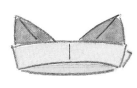

4 The G.I. Cap ■ complete. To make a full-sized cap, use a square trimmed from a large format newspaper.

■ S T A R

The shape made in Step 7 is known in origami as the Preliminary Base, so called because other, more advanced bases can be developed from it, including the Bird and Frog bases and their stretched variants. Use a square of paper or perhaps paper-backed foil, coloured side up.

Designed by Florence Temko, USA.

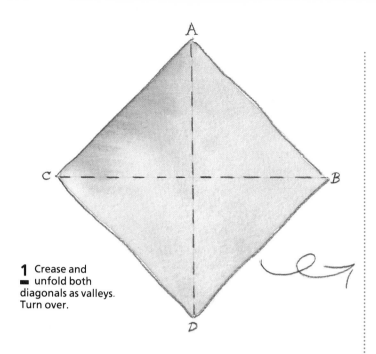

1 Crease and unfold both diagonals as valleys. Turn over.

2 Check that the diagonals are now mountain creases.

3 Fold and unfold in half down the middle, then . . .

4 . . . fold in half across the middle.

5 Hold as shown. If the mountain and valley creases have been placed correctly, a 3D diamond shape will emerge when the hands are swung towards each other . . .

6 . . . like this. Flatten G against E and F against H.

7 Fold the single layer corner C up to I, then unfold.

(Continued . . .)

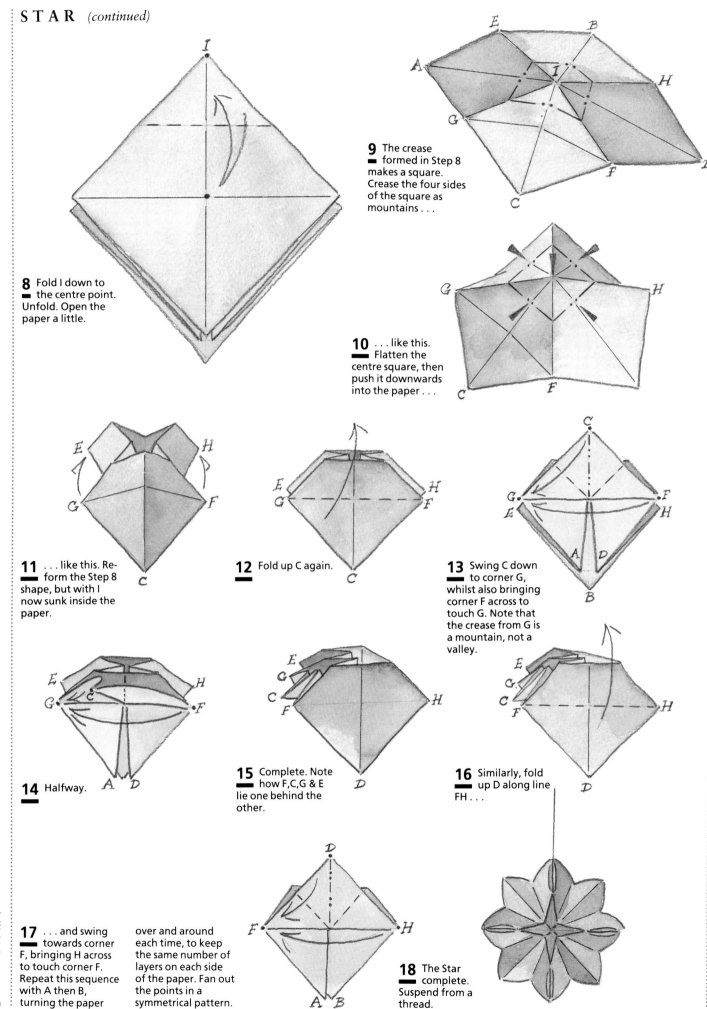

8 Fold I down to the centre point. Unfold. Open the paper a little.

9 The crease formed in Step 8 makes a square. Crease the four sides of the square as mountains . . .

10 . . . like this. Flatten the centre square, then push it downwards into the paper . . .

11 . . . like this. Re-form the Step 8 shape, but with I now sunk inside the paper.

12 Fold up C again.

13 Swing C down to corner G, whilst also bringing corner F across to touch G. Note that the crease from G is a mountain, not a valley.

14 Halfway.

15 Complete. Note how F, C, G & E lie one behind the other.

16 Similarly, fold up D along line FH . . .

17 . . . and swing towards corner F, bringing H across to touch corner F. Repeat this sequence with A then B, turning the paper over and around each time, to keep the same number of layers on each side of the paper. Fan out the points in a symmetrical pattern.

18 The Star complete. Suspend from a thread.

INTERMEDIATE PROJECTS

Many people – particularly
mischievous children – have learnt how
to make a waterbomb, but without
practice, it is very easy to forget how to
lock it. Without a good lock, it cannot
contain the water it is designed to hold!
More peaceably, it makes an excellent
Christmas decoration if folded from a
patterned paper. Use a square of paper.
If using origami paper, start with the
white side uppermost.

Traditional design.

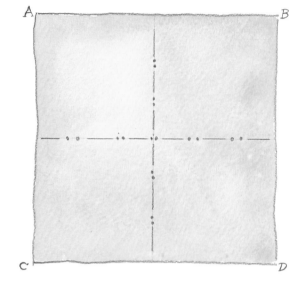

1 Mountain fold
■ horizontally and
vertically across the
paper. Unfold each
time.

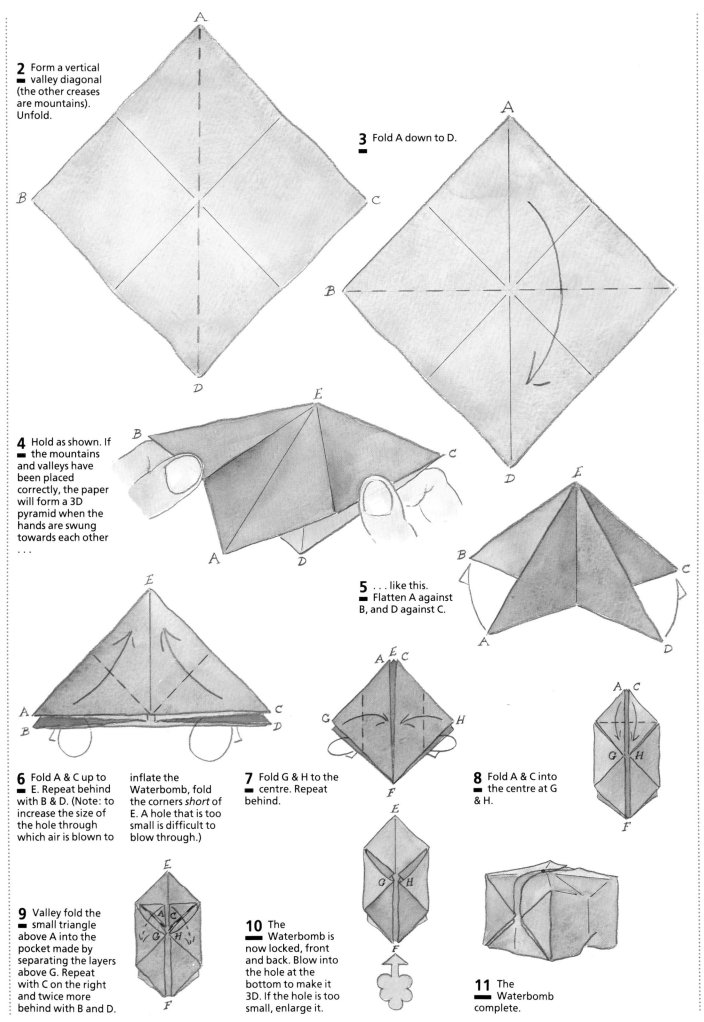

2 Form a vertical valley diagonal (the other creases are mountains). Unfold.

3 Fold A down to D.

4 Hold as shown. If the mountains and valleys have been placed correctly, the paper will form a 3D pyramid when the hands are swung towards each other . . .

5 . . . like this. Flatten A against B, and D against C.

6 Fold A & C up to E. Repeat behind with B & D. (Note: to increase the size of the hole through which air is blown to inflate the Waterbomb, fold the corners *short* of E. A hole that is too small is difficult to blow through.)

7 Fold G & H to the centre. Repeat behind.

8 Fold A & C into the centre at G & H.

9 Valley fold the small triangle above A into the pocket made by separating the layers above G. Repeat with C on the right and twice more behind with B and D.

10 The Waterbomb is now locked, front and back. Blow into the hole at the bottom to make it 3D. If the hole is too small, enlarge it.

11 The Waterbomb complete.

TRADITIONAL BOX

This is perhaps *the* classic origami box. It is quick and simple to make, and locks strongly. A box made from a slightly larger square will form a lid. In Step 3, if the creases are not placed at the quarter points, but elsewhere, taller or squatter boxes can be made. Use a square of strong paper. If using origami paper, start white side up.

Traditional design.

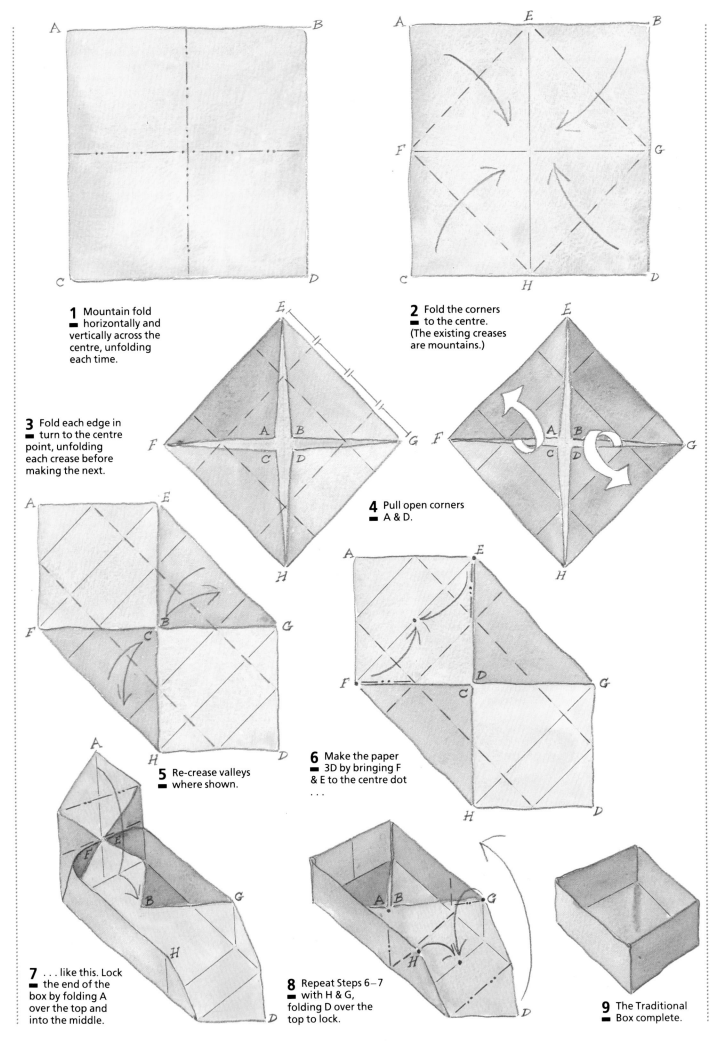

1 Mountain fold horizontally and vertically across the centre, unfolding each time.

2 Fold the corners to the centre. (The existing creases are mountains.)

3 Fold each edge in turn to the centre point, unfolding each crease before making the next.

4 Pull open corners A & D.

5 Re-crease valleys where shown.

6 Make the paper 3D by bringing F & E to the centre dot . . .

7 . . . like this. Lock the end of the box by folding A over the top and into the middle.

8 Repeat Steps 6–7 with H & G, folding D over the top to lock.

9 The Traditional Box complete.

The design features a peculiar and little-used manoeuvre at Steps 4–5, when one spike is pulled out from inside another that envelops it. The move is very satisfying! What was a closed and rather unpromising shape in Step 4 becomes much more useful by Step 6, yet no new creases are made. Begin with a square of paper, same colour both sides.

Designed by Paul Jackson.

A

B ---- **C**

D

1 Crease and
■ unfold a vertical
diagonal, then fold
D up to A.

D A

B

C

2 Fold edges AD,B
■ and AD,C to the
centre crease.

D A

B **C**

3 Fold out corners B
■ & C.

D A

B **C**

4 Note the shape of
■ the paper. Pull
out D from inside A
. . .

A **D**

B **C**

5 . . . like this.
■ Flatten D on top
of A.

A **D**

B **C**

6 Turn over.

A **D**

B **C**

7 Collapse the
■ paper as shown,
separating A from D
and bringing C to
touch B.

D **A**

C
B

8 Lift up corner C,
■ squashing the
paper flat at the left.

D **A**

C

B

9 Fold B behind.

D **A**

B

C

10 Reverse fold D.
■ Fold out the
bottom corners to
stay away from the
wings and so create
a stable base for the
bird to balance on.

11 The Nesting
■ Bird complete.

This is a variation on a well-known origami 'action' theme. The mechanism will be familiar to knowledgeable paper folders, but here the eyes are made differently. It is important to use origami paper, to achieve a contrast of colour for the eyes and the inside of the mouth. The colour should be on the outside in Step 1.

Designed by Paul Jackson.

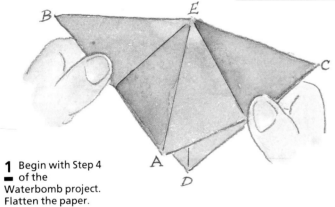

1 Begin with Step 4 of the Waterbomb project. Flatten the paper.

2 Fold B & C to E.

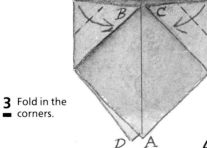

3 Fold in the corners.

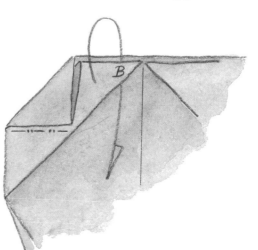

4 (The instructions now refer to B only, but repeat all Steps with C.) Swivel B behind and downwards . . .

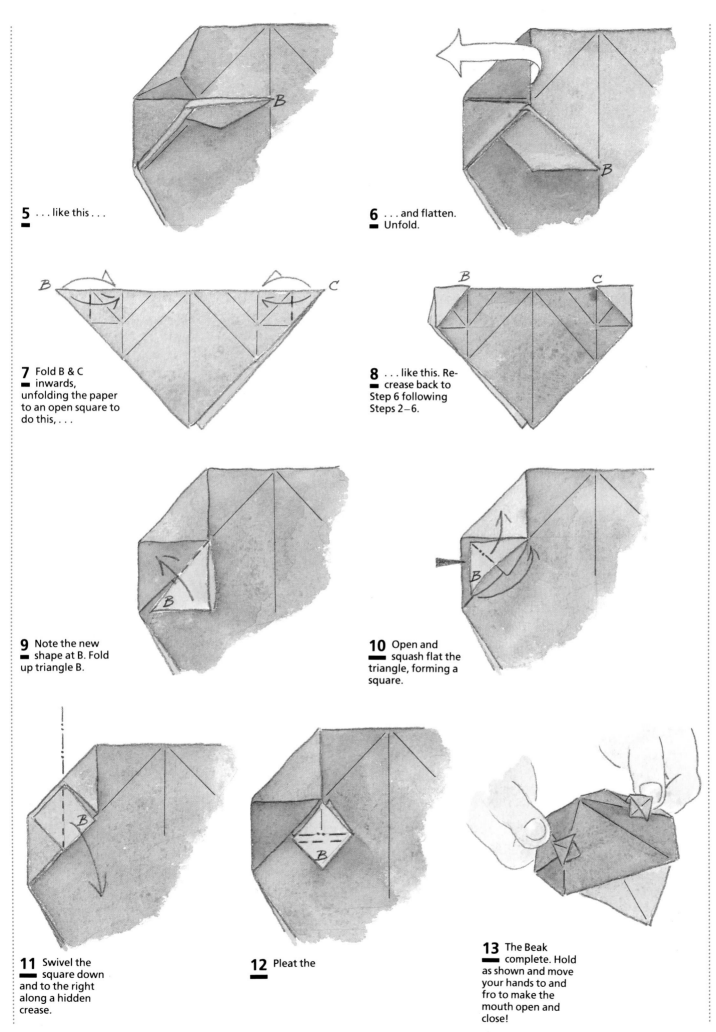

5 . . . like this . . .

6 . . . and flatten. Unfold.

7 Fold B & C inwards, unfolding the paper to an open square to do this, . . .

8 . . . like this. Recrease back to Step 6 following Steps 2–6.

9 Note the new shape at B. Fold up triangle B.

10 Open and squash flat the triangle, forming a square.

11 Swivel the square down and to the right along a hidden crease.

12 Pleat the

13 The Beak complete. Hold as shown and move your hands to and fro to make the mouth open and close!

▌L I G H T H E A R T E D

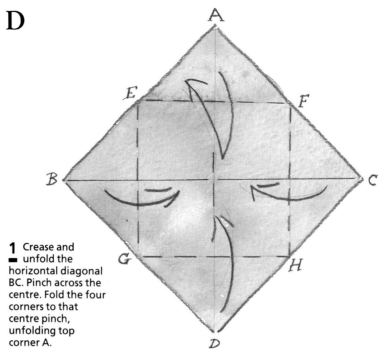

Original concepts are rare in origami. Most designs, however good, are created within relatively predictable themes, so it is pleasing to occasionally find a fresh approach. In this design, the final shape is unimpressive, but reveals a translucent heart when held against the light! Fold the paper carefully, particularly at Steps 2–3, or the heart will be poorly proportioned. Use a square of thin paper; thicker papers will not reveal the heart.

Designed by Wayne Brown, UK.

1 Crease and unfold the horizontal diagonal BC. Pinch across the centre. Fold the four corners to that centre pinch, unfolding top corner A.

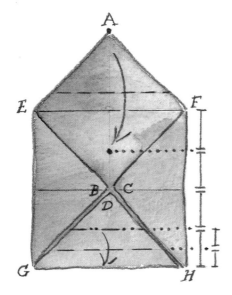

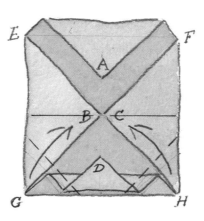

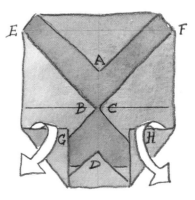

2 Fold down corner A as shown. Pleat triangle DGH as shown.

3 Fold in corners G & H. Note the very small intrusion of the crease into the D triangle. This is important, as it affects the proportion of the heart.

4 Unfold Step 3.

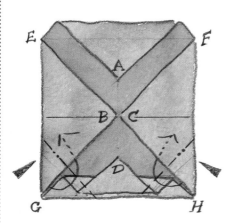

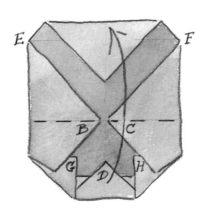

5 Re-crease Step 3, but reverse folding the top part of each crease to push G under B, and H under C.

6 Fold in half.

7 Fold in E & F just a little way.

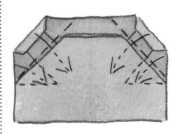

8 Fold over as shown, locking the edges into the pockets made in Step 5.

9 Fold the excess paper into the top pocket.

10 Note that the shape is locked flat.

11 To see the heart, hold the paper up to a window or other diffuse light source (but not the sun).

▮ STAR BOX

This is one of the simpler decorative origami boxes. It is relatively easy to make a square, straight-sided box, such as the Traditional Box project, but the technical complexities increase as the final shape becomes less plain. Here though, the design is pleasingly bold. Use a square of origami paper, with the coloured side outwards.

Traditional design.

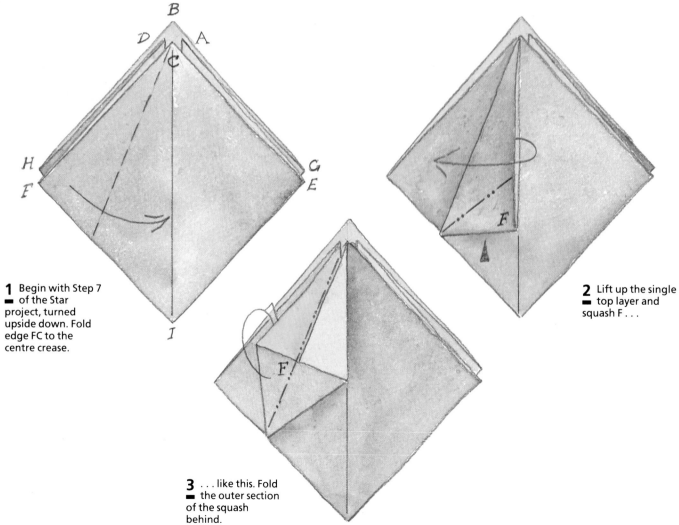

1 Begin with Step 7 of the Star project, turned upside down. Fold edge FC to the centre crease.

2 Lift up the single top layer and squash F . . .

3 . . . like this. Fold the outer section of the squash behind.

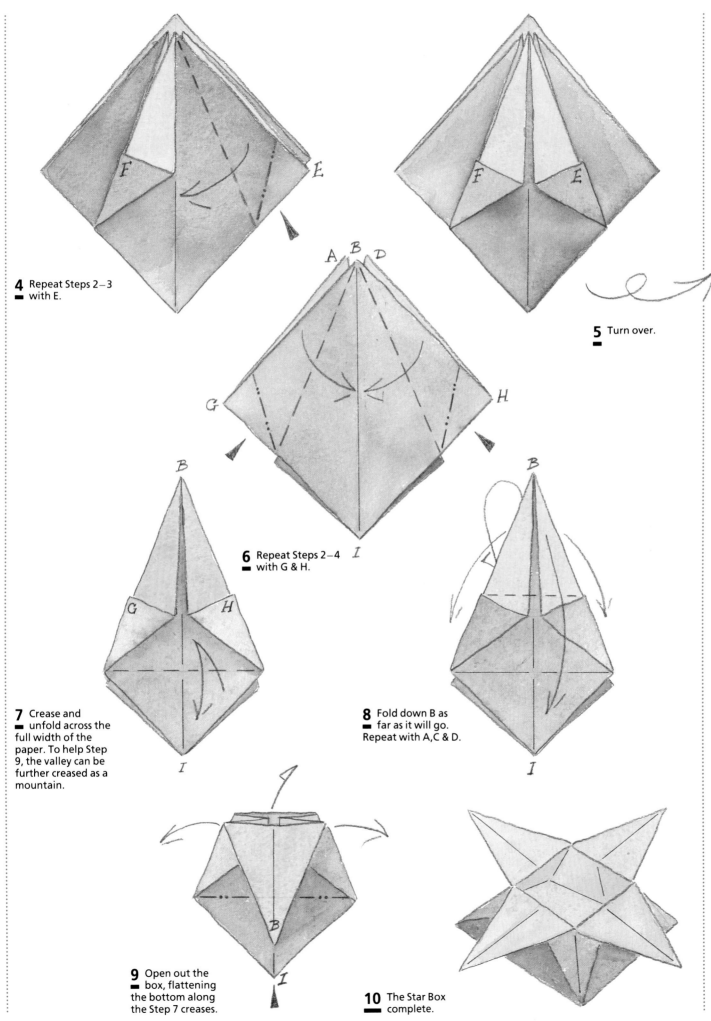

4 Repeat Steps 2–3 with E.

5 Turn over.

6 Repeat Steps 2–4 with G & H.

7 Crease and unfold across the full width of the paper. To help Step 9, the valley can be further creased as a mountain.

8 Fold down B as far as it will go. Repeat with A, C & D.

9 Open out the box, flattening the bottom along the Step 7 creases.

10 The Star Box complete.

JUMPING FROG

There are many origami jumping frogs, most – like this one – made by creating a frog shape, then pleating across the body to create the spring. This version is a particularly athletic jumper. Use a 20 cm (8 in) square of paper. A 2 × 1 rectangle of thick paper may also be used, starting at Step 2.

Traditional design.

1 Fold a square in half down the middle.

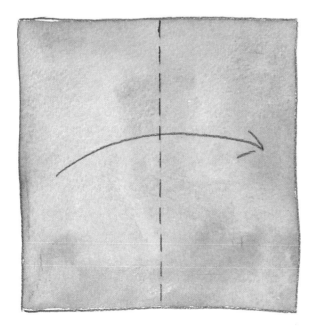

2 The paper is now two layers thick, but will be referred to as though it was a single layer. Collapse AB to make the shape seen in Step 6 of the Waterbomb project.

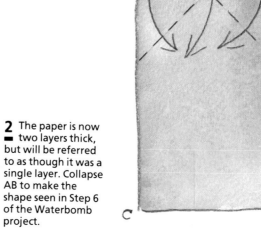

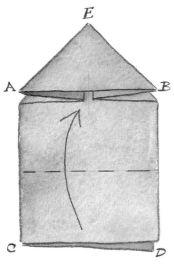

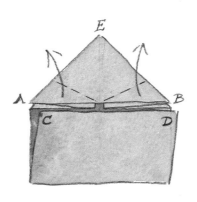

4 Swing out A & B.
■ Note that they do not touch E, but protrude to the side.

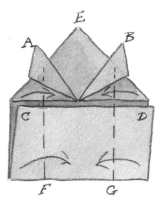

5 Fold in the sides.

3 Fold up edge CD
■ to AB.

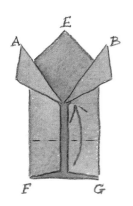

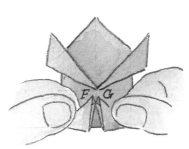

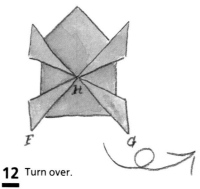

7 Fold down
■ corners F & G . . .

8 . . . like this.

9 Hold tightly as
■ shown. Slide F & G away from H . . .

6 Fold edge FG to
■ the centre point.

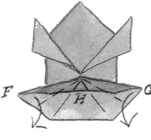

10 . . . like this,
■ keeping firm hold of F & G. When F & G have been pulled out as far to the side as they will go, flatten the paper . . .

11 . . . like this.
■ Fold down F & G.

12 Turn over.

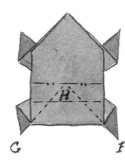

13 Make a pleat,
■ with the mountain crease passing through H. The paper is very thick, so use considerable pressure.

14 The Jumping
■ Frog complete.

15 To make it
■ jump, put your finger on its back. Flatten the pleat and slide your finger off! With practice, it will jump quite a distance.

BIRD

This design is straightforward until
Step 9, when the difficult 3D crimp
transforms an ordinary flat bird into a
3D bird with a pleasingly rounded
shape. Some origami creators argue
that such '3D-ing' at the end of the
folding sequence is a cheat, and that a
truly 3D design is folded as such from
the start. Use a 15–20 cm (6–8 in)
square of paper, coloured the same on
both sides.

Designed by Paul Jackson.

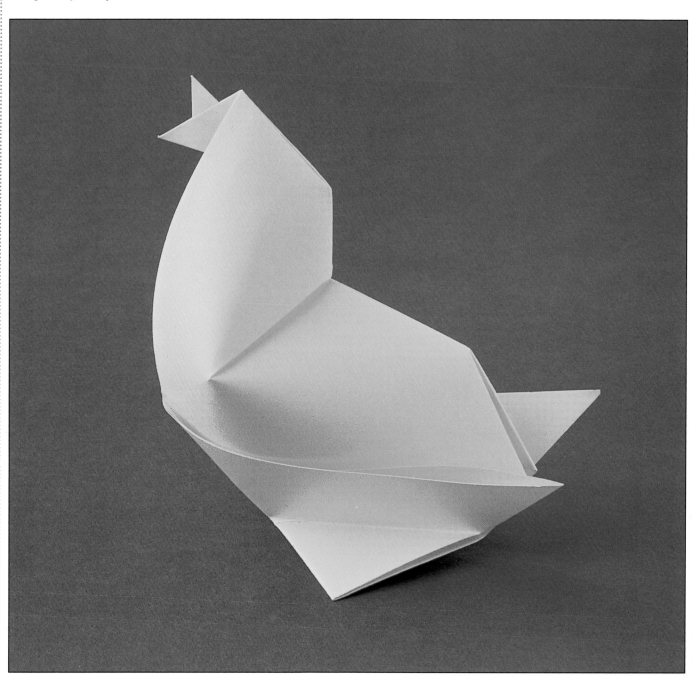

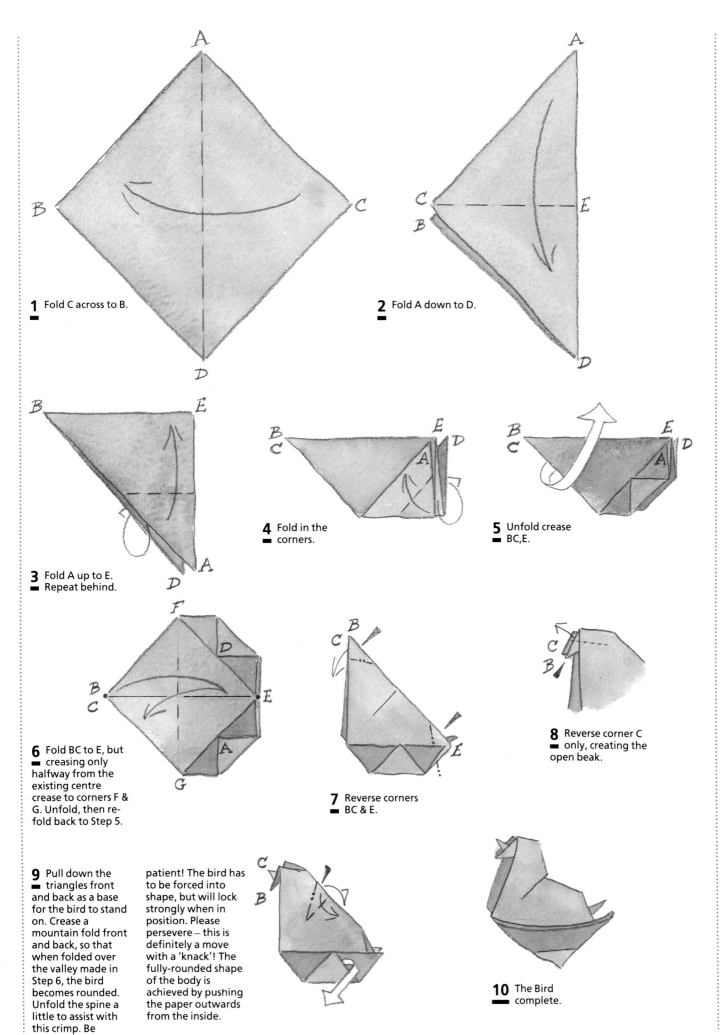

1 Fold C across to B.

2 Fold A down to D.

3 Fold A up to E. Repeat behind.

4 Fold in the corners.

5 Unfold crease BC,E.

6 Fold BC to E, but creasing only halfway from the existing centre crease to corners F & G. Unfold, then re-fold back to Step 5.

7 Reverse corners BC & E.

8 Reverse corner C only, creating the open beak.

9 Pull down the triangles front and back as a base for the bird to stand on. Crease a mountain fold front and back, so that when folded over the valley made in Step 6, the bird becomes rounded. Unfold the spine a little to assist with this crimp. Be patient! The bird has to be forced into shape, but will lock strongly when in position. Please persevere – this is definitely a move with a 'knack'! The fully-rounded shape of the body is achieved by pushing the paper outwards from the inside.

10 The Bird complete.

BUILDING

The design is included in the book to
show how the rectangles and triangles
that are created naturally by folding a
square along halves and quarters, can
be articulated to create a form such as
this semi-abstract building, complete
with colour-change roofs. Often,
allowing the paper to do what it wants
to do without contrivance is the best
way to create. Use a square of origami
paper, white side up.

Designed by Paul Jackson.

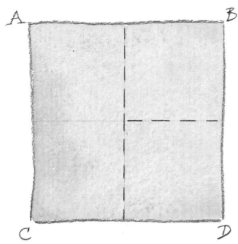

1 Crease as shown. Note the short crease at the right.

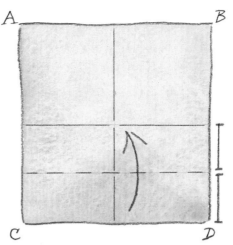

2 Fold edge CD up to the centre crease, then fold in half down the middle.

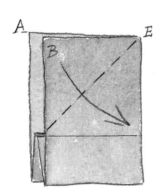

3 Fold down corner B.

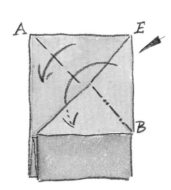

4 Reverse fold corner E behind B.

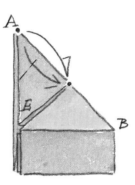

5 Fold corner A as shown, opening the paper to do this.

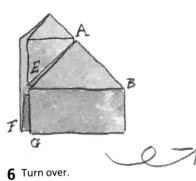

6 Turn over.

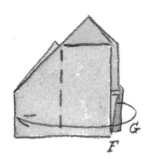

7 Swing F over to the left.

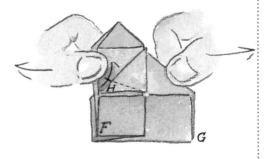

8 Hold as shown and move your hands apart. Corner H will lift. Crease and flatten H as shown . . .

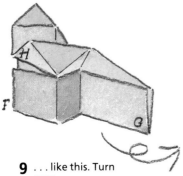

9 . . . like this. Turn over.

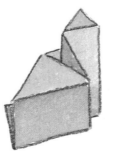

10 The Building complete.

PIG

The Pig, although a fairly complex project, is rewarding to construct, especially as the finished animal emerges in the final steps. Take time over the snout folds – they may appear complicated but do give a realistic result. Choose a 'pig'-coloured paper and use a 2 × 1 rectangle, the same colour on both sides. It is easy to create a whole 'family' of origami pigs: simply vary the size of the initial 2 × 1 rectangle.

Designed by Paul Jackson.

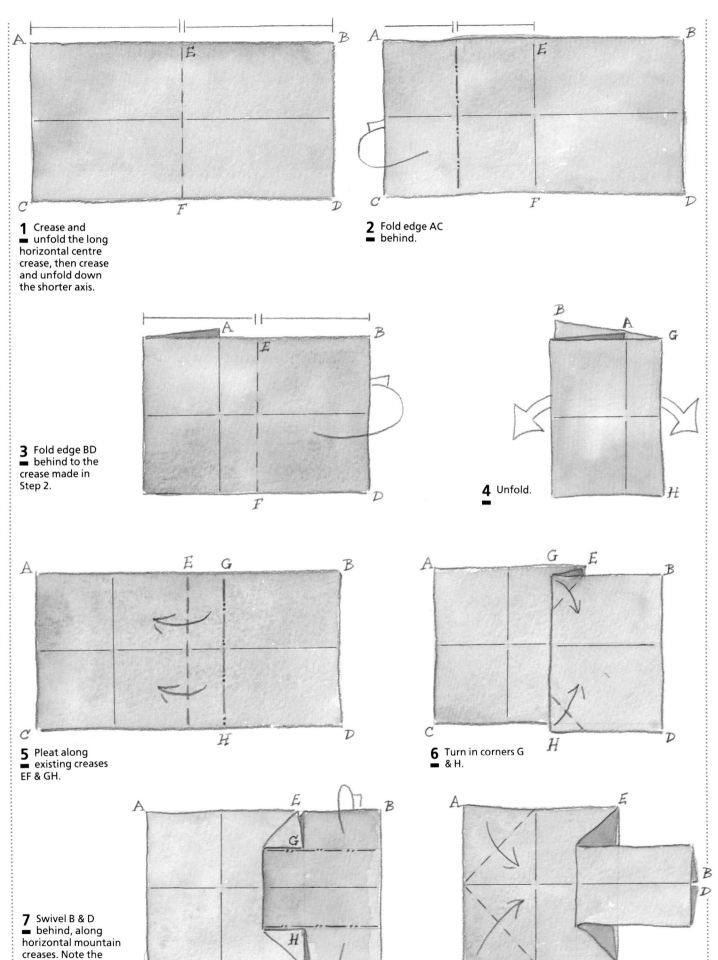

1 Crease and unfold the long horizontal centre crease, then crease and unfold down the shorter axis.

2 Fold edge AC behind.

3 Fold edge BD behind to the crease made in Step 2.

4 Unfold.

5 Pleat along existing creases EF & GH.

6 Turn in corners G & H.

7 Swivel B & D behind, along horizontal mountain creases. Note the shape of Step 8.

8 Fold in corners A & C.

(continued . . .)

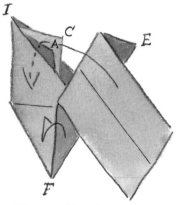

9 Fold A & C back out, the creases tapering towards I.

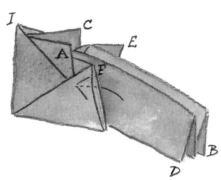

10 Collapse as shown, to make the paper 3D.

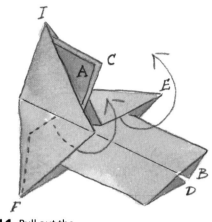

11 Pull out the hidden ledge . . .

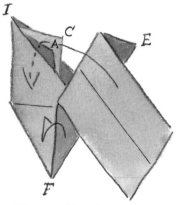

12 . . . and feed it back into the pig between A & C . . .

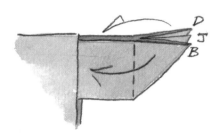

13 . . . like this, bringing F & E back together again.

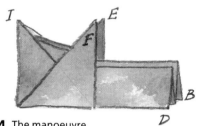

14 The manoeuvre is complete – its purpose is to stop the pig from splaying its front legs. Turn the paper the right way up.

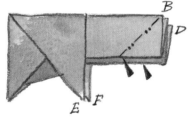

15 Reverse fold at B & D.

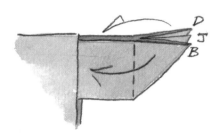

16 Fold B & D towards the neck.

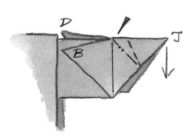

17 Create two reverse folds near the snout, forming a crimp.

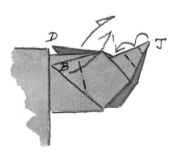

18 Fold the snout over and over. Fold the ears forward.

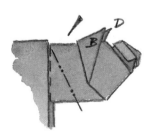

19 Crimp the neck, lowering the head.

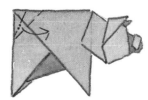

20 Pleat the tail.

21 The Pig complete.

■ STANDING HEART

Hearts are a favourite origami theme,
particularly when combined with
another element, such as a heart
pierced by an arrow, twin hearts or a
heart on a finger ring. Here is a
conventional single heart, but one
which could make an attractive
standing ornament for a mantelpiece or
desk top. Use a square of red/white
origami paper, red side up.

Designed by Paul Jackson.

(Continued . . .)

1 Crease and unfold across the middle, then fold AC across to BD.

2 Mountain fold corners C & D inside.

3 Squash fold corner E.

4 Fold the outer section of the squash fold behind.

5 Open the paper between G & H. Turn over to see . . .

6 . . . a pyramid. Corner I is the apex (the corner nearest to you). Push on I so that it inverts and the paper pops inside out. Corner I is now the furthest point from you, not the nearest.

7 This is the shape. Note I.

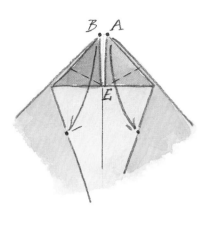

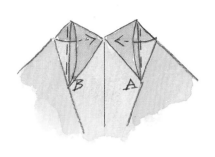

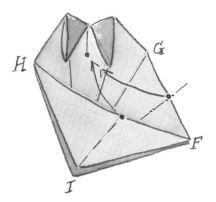

8 Fold down B & A, dot to dot.

9 Tuck the excess paper into the pockets at B & A.

10 Collapse as shown, folding the two outer dots onto the inner one.

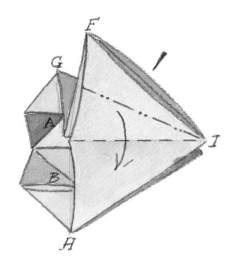

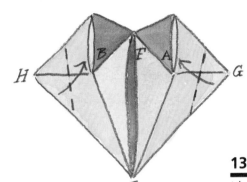

11 Squash F, presently standing upright.

12 Fold in H & G.

13 Fold over G to lock the triangle to the edge behind.

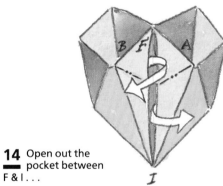

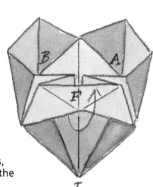

14 Open out the pocket between F & I . . .

15 . . . like this, flattening the paper.

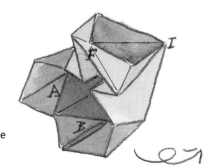

16 Partly close the pocket again. Turn over.

17 The Standing Heart complete.

FIGHTER JET

There are purists who may cry 'cheat' at this design, because it is made from two pieces of paper. A near-identical one-piece version from a 3 × 2 rectangle post-dated this original design, but is messy to make and lacks the simplicity of the original. Use two identical squares of paper of the same size and colour, coloured the same on both sides.

Designed by Paul Jackson.

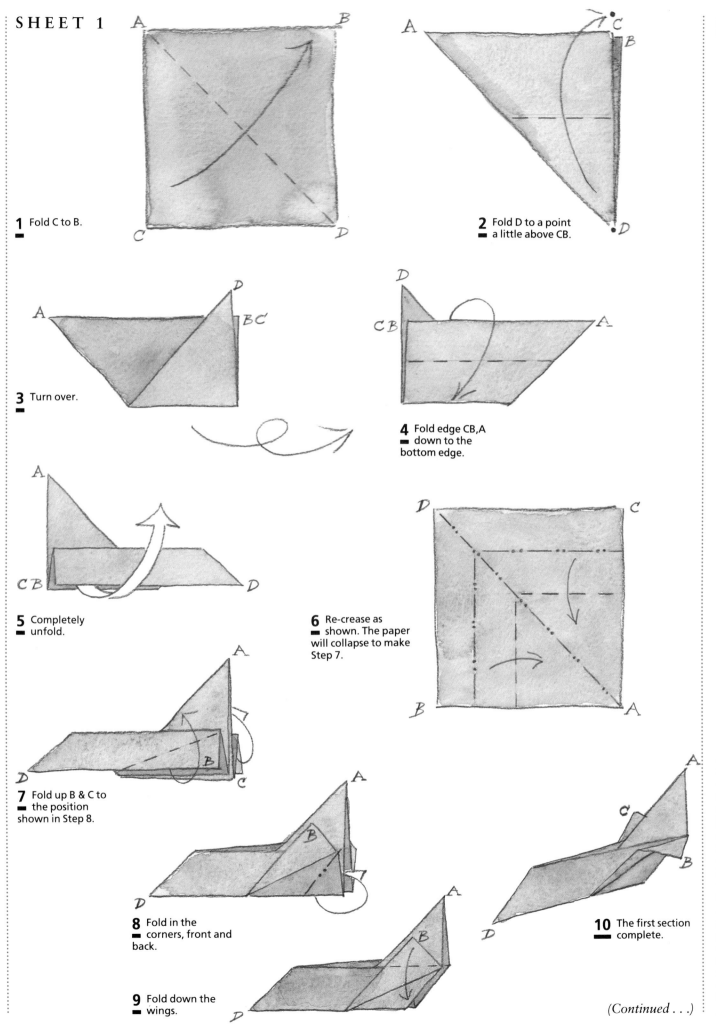

SHEET 1

1 Fold C to B.

2 Fold D to a point a little above CB.

3 Turn over.

4 Fold edge CB,A down to the bottom edge.

5 Completely unfold.

6 Re-crease as shown. The paper will collapse to make Step 7.

7 Fold up B & C to the position shown in Step 8.

8 Fold in the corners, front and back.

9 Fold down the wings.

10 The first section complete.

(Continued . . .)

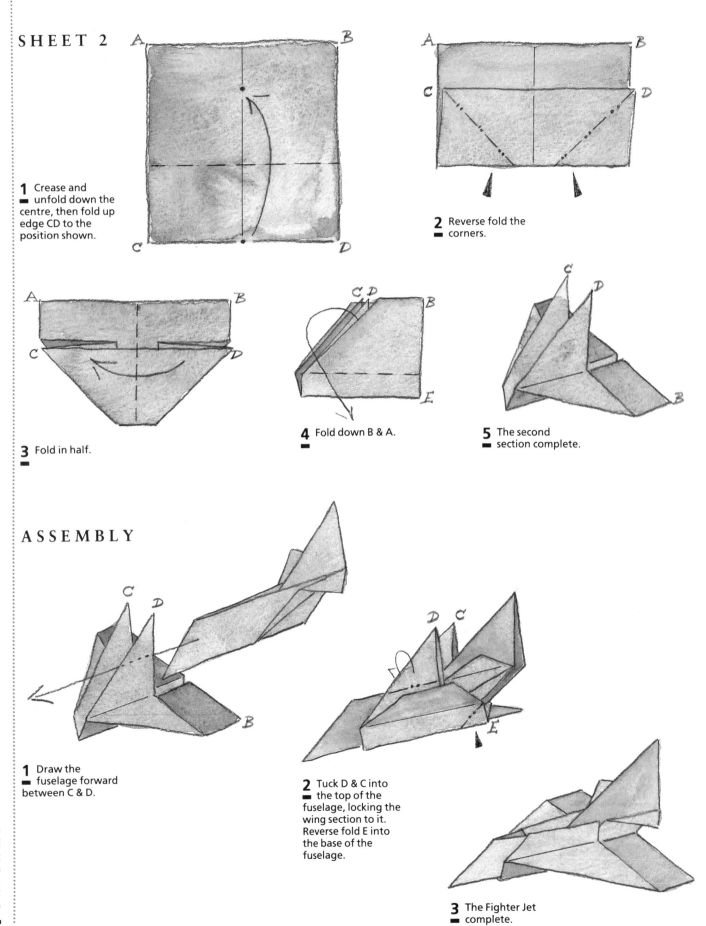

SHEET 2

1 Crease and unfold down the centre, then fold up edge CD to the position shown.

2 Reverse fold the corners.

3 Fold in half.

4 Fold down B & A.

5 The second section complete.

ASSEMBLY

1 Draw the fuselage forward between C & D.

2 Tuck D & C into the top of the fuselage, locking the wing section to it. Reverse fold E into the base of the fuselage.

3 The Fighter Jet complete.

ADVANCED PROJECTS

CAMEL

The shape formed in Step 5 is commonly known in origami as the Fish base, and for obvious reasons. Apart from fishes (and a camel), the base at Step 6 is ideally shaped to create many different birds – the blunt points make wings and the sharp points form a head and tail. Use a 15–20 cm (6–8 in) square of paper, same colour both sides.

Designed by Paul Jackson.

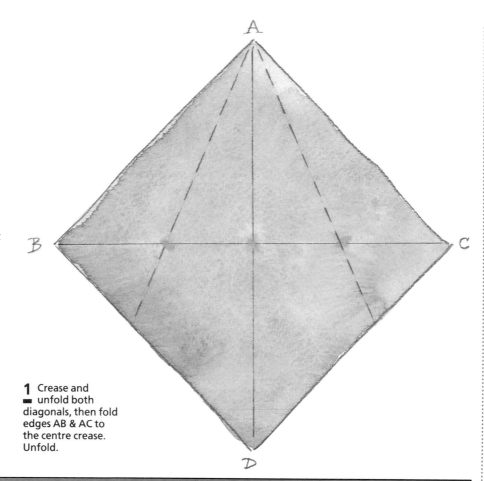

1 Crease and unfold both diagonals, then fold edges AB & AC to the centre crease. Unfold.

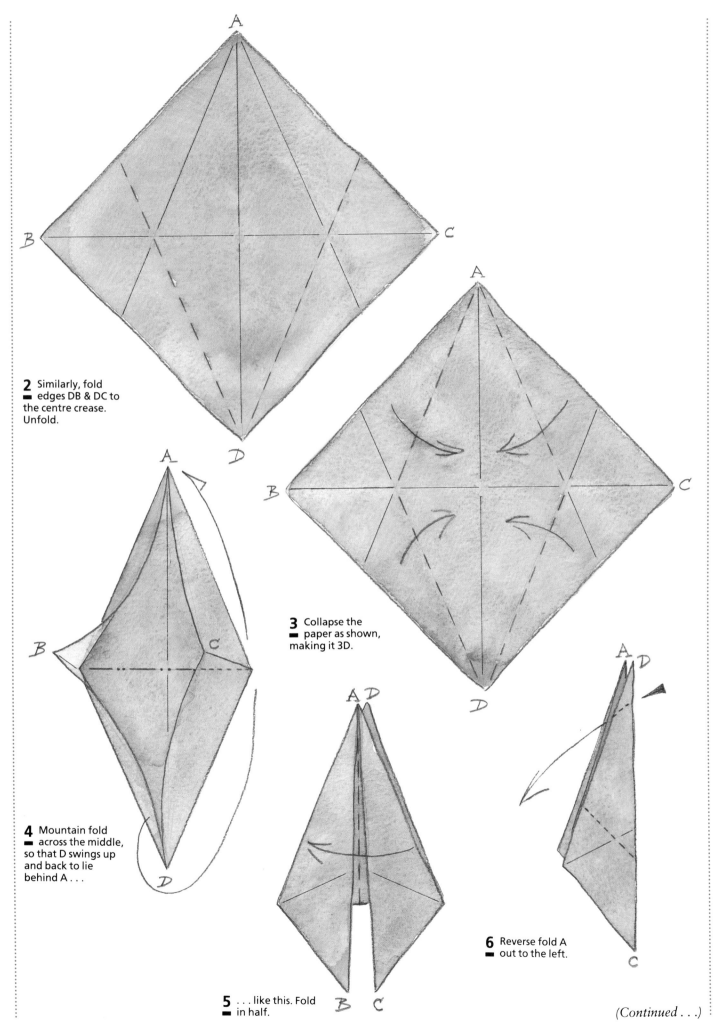

2 Similarly, fold edges DB & DC to the centre crease. Unfold.

3 Collapse the paper as shown, making it 3D.

4 Mountain fold across the middle, so that D swings up and back to lie behind A . . .

5 . . . like this. Fold in half.

6 Reverse fold A out to the left.

(Continued . . .)

7 Crease and unfold three creases which bisect the angles of the large triangle. The creases should all meet at a common point. Repeat behind.

8 Re-crease front and back, collapsing the paper . . .

9 . . . to this shape. Outside reverse fold D.

10 Outside reverse fold A & D.

11 Release the layers at A & D. At A, fold the released layers back over the legs. At D, allow the layers to remain visible, increasing the width of the head.

12 Fold the central layer in half to lock the hump shut.

13 This is the shape at the back.

14 Reverse fold D inside.

15 Turn the muzzle inside out.

16 The Camel complete.

CHINESE VASE

This wonderful design was first introduced to the West by Dr Philip Shen (whose bowl appears earlier) and popularized in the USA by the late Verdi Adams. It has a beautifully direct sequence of folds, climaxed by the extraordinary opening out from 2D to 3D. Use a square of paper, not too small. If using origami paper, start white side up.

Traditional design.

(Continued . . .)

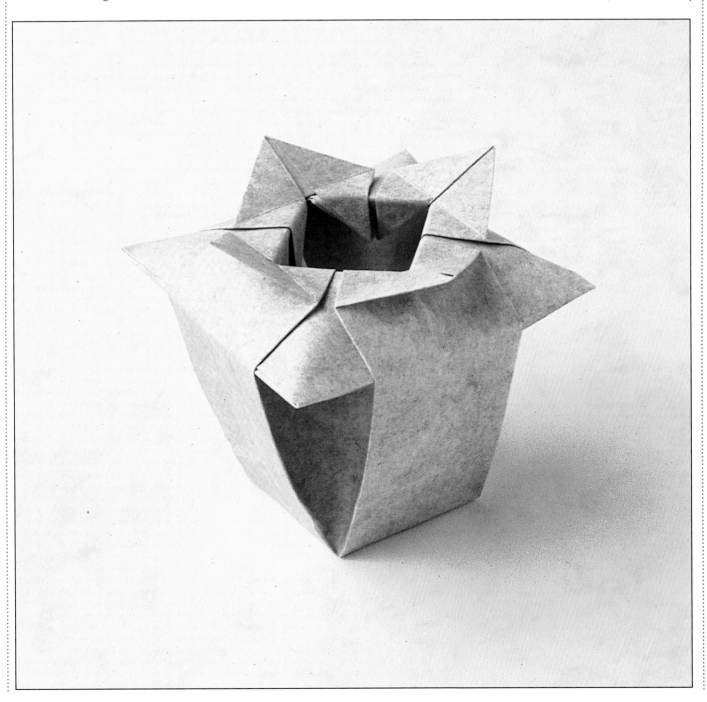

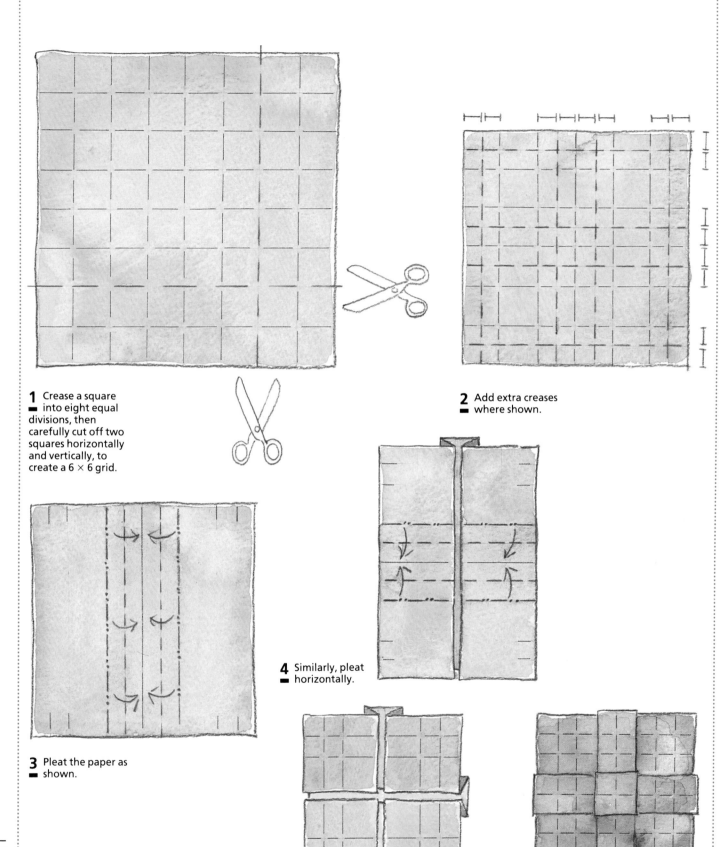

1 Crease a square
into eight equal
divisions, then
carefully cut off two
squares horizontally
and vertically, to
create a 6 × 6 grid.

2 Add extra creases
where shown.

3 Pleat the paper as
shown.

4 Similarly, pleat
horizontally.

5 This is the shape
of the paper.
Turn over.

6 This is the shape.

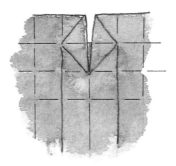

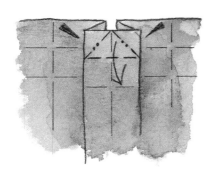

7 Lift and squash the end of each pleat . . .

8 . . . like this.

9 Repeat along each edge.

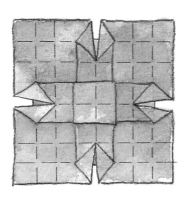

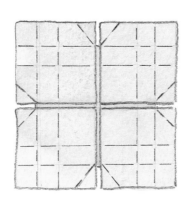

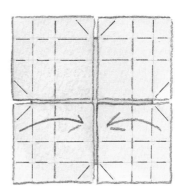

10 Here are the squashed pleats. Turn over.

11 Crease and unfold each loose corner at the pleats. This is to prepare for Step 14.

12 Fold the sides to the middle.

13 Fold the top and bottom edges to the middle, tucking the corners deep into the pockets.

14 Fold the loose corners inside, to create a square opening . . .

15 . . . like this. Turn over.

16 This is the fun part! Carefully tease out the trapped layers inside the pleats to make the vase 3D. Do this by rotating the paper frequently, so that all four sides are developed equally.

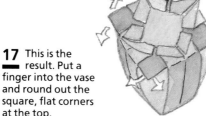

17 This is the result. Put a finger into the vase and round out the square, flat corners at the top.

18 The Chinese Vase complete.

SEATED FIGURE

One of the delights of origami is its ability to conjure complex subjects from relatively simple folds, to create not a detailed representation, but a stylized abstraction. When successful, the result is poetic, both in concept and form. Use a square of origami paper, coloured side up.

Designed by Paul Jackson.

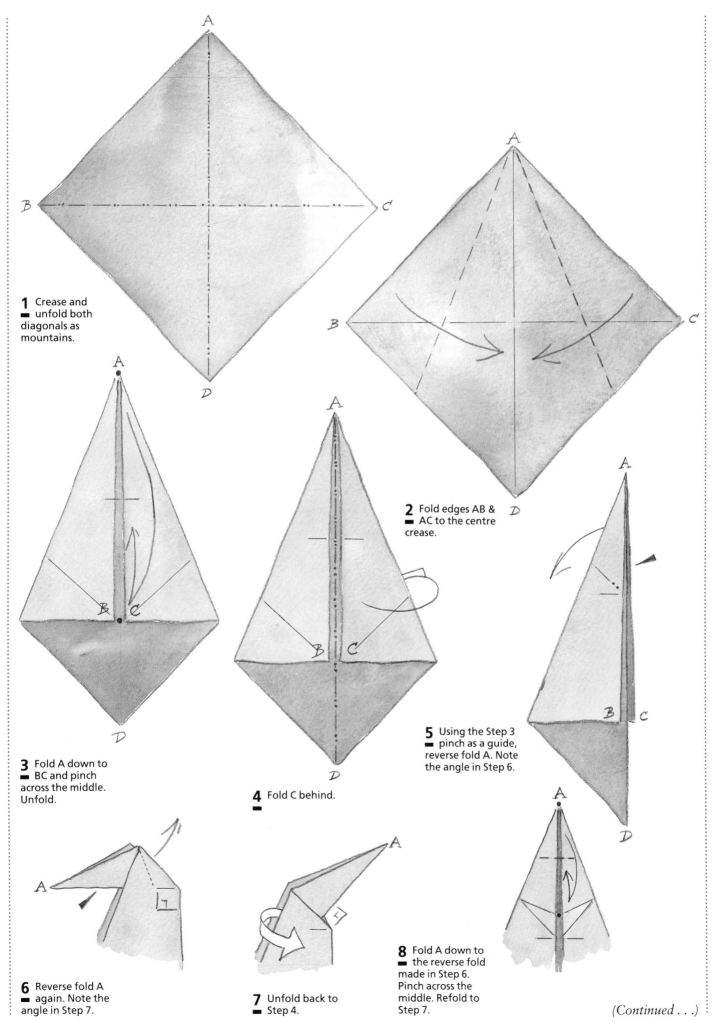

1 Crease and unfold both diagonals as mountains.

2 Fold edges AB & AC to the centre crease.

3 Fold A down to BC and pinch across the middle. Unfold.

4 Fold C behind.

5 Using the Step 3 pinch as a guide, reverse fold A. Note the angle in Step 6.

6 Reverse fold A again. Note the angle in Step 7.

7 Unfold back to Step 4.

8 Fold A down to the reverse fold made in Step 6. Pinch across the middle. Refold to Step 7.

(Continued . . .)

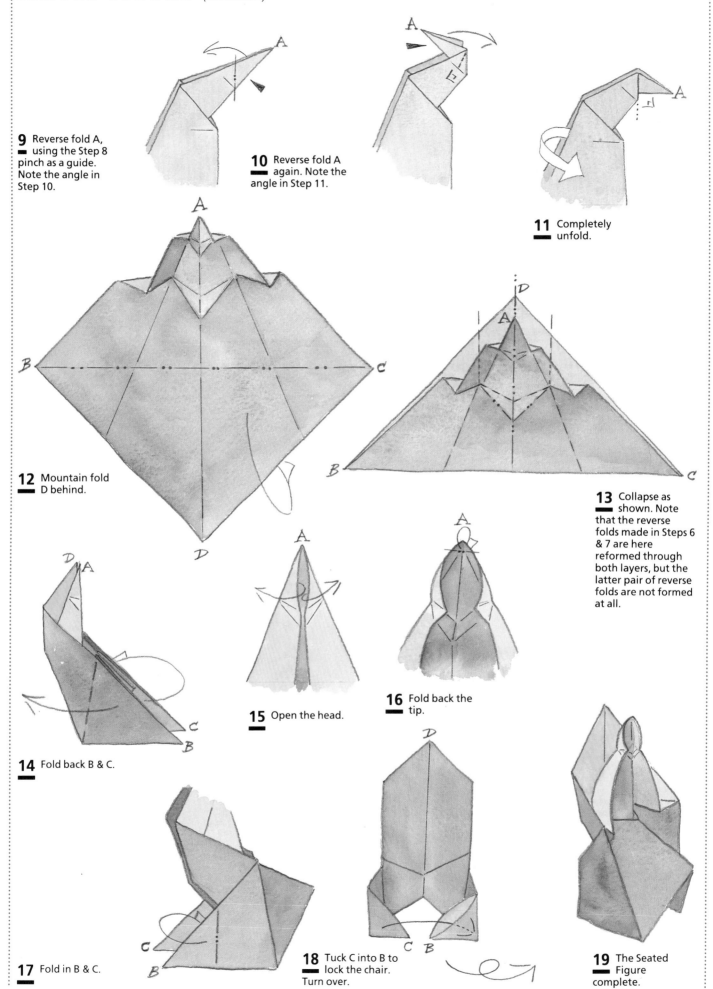

9 Reverse fold A, using the Step 8 pinch as a guide. Note the angle in Step 10.

10 Reverse fold A again. Note the angle in Step 11.

11 Completely unfold.

12 Mountain fold D behind.

13 Collapse as shown. Note that the reverse folds made in Steps 6 & 7 are here reformed through both layers, but the latter pair of reverse folds are not formed at all.

14 Fold back B & C.

15 Open the head.

16 Fold back the tip.

17 Fold in B & C.

18 Tuck C into B to lock the chair. Turn over.

19 The Seated Figure complete.

∎ ELECTRA

An appeal of modular folding is that
spectacular structures can be made
from simple units, so that the whole is
very much more than the sum of its
parts. Thirty modules are needed for
this design, which will take about an
hour to make. Fold them all very
carefully, then slot them together, with
diligent regard for the '5 and 3'
(pentagons and triangles) interlocking
pattern. The result is a pierced
structure of great beauty and strength.
Use 30 10 cm (4 in) squares.
If using origami paper, start with the
coloured side up.

Designed by David Mitchell, UK.

(Continued . . .)

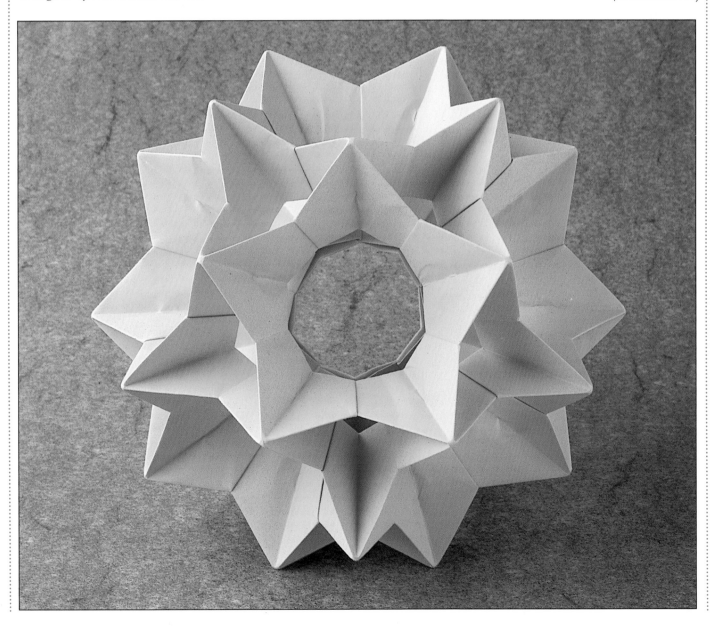

METHOD

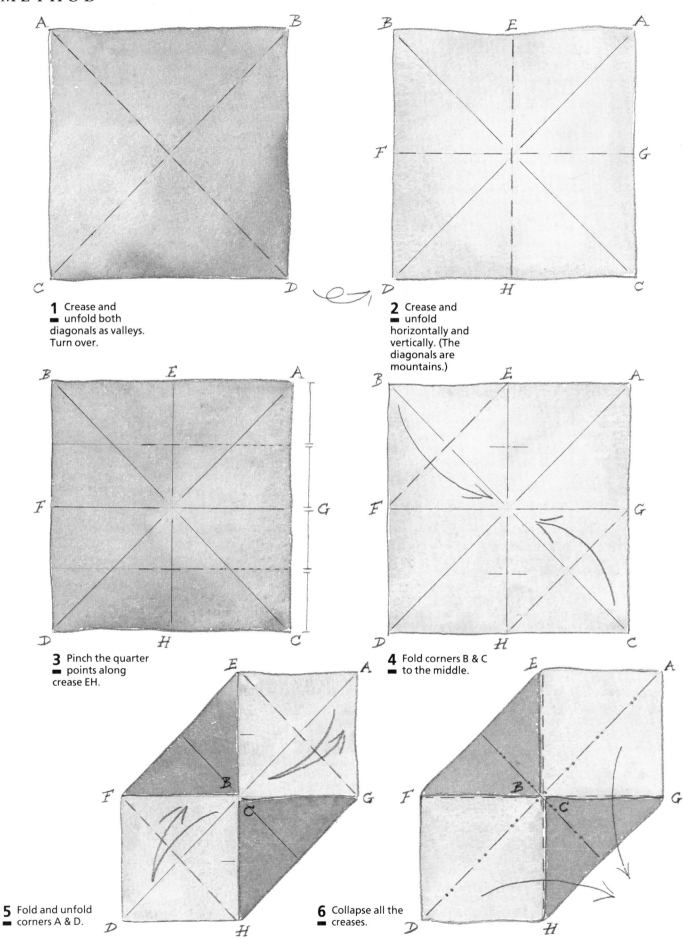

1 Crease and unfold both diagonals as valleys. Turn over.

2 Crease and unfold horizontally and vertically. (The diagonals are mountains.)

3 Pinch the quarter points along crease EH.

4 Fold corners B & C to the middle.

5 Fold and unfold corners A & D.

6 Collapse all the creases.

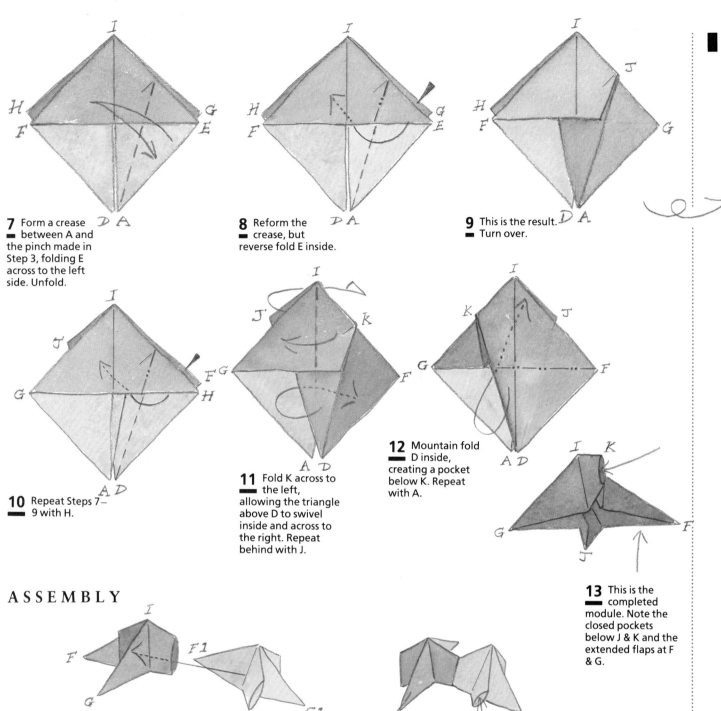

7 Form a crease between A and the pinch made in Step 3, folding E across to the left side. Unfold.

8 Reform the crease, but reverse fold E inside.

9 This is the result. Turn over.

10 Repeat Steps 7–9 with H.

11 Fold K across to the left, allowing the triangle above D to swivel inside and across to the right. Repeat behind with J.

12 Mountain fold D inside, creating a pocket below K. Repeat with A.

13 This is the completed module. Note the closed pockets below J & K and the extended flaps at F & G.

ASSEMBLY

1 Tuck the extended flap on one module (F1), deep inside the pocket of another. To lock them together, fold F or G (depending on which one flap F1 has been tucked into) towards G1.

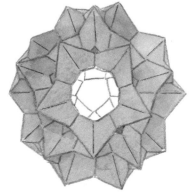

2 Repeat with the nearside flaps and pockets.

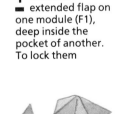
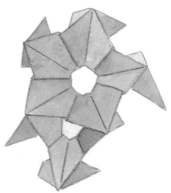

3 Lock 5 modules together, leaving no excess flaps in the centre of the pentagon. A sixth module is shown at the very bottom of the drawing connecting two neighbouring pentagon modules, thereby creating a triangle with no loose flaps in its centre. The completed Electra is thus a combination of pentagons and triangles. Interlock the remaining modules following this pattern.

4 The completed Electra.

■ SEAL ON A ROCK

So called 'double subjects' or 'combination folds' are common in complex origami, where two subjects or objects are folded from a single sheet. Examples might include a mother pushing a pram, a man playing an instrument or, as in this case, a seal basking on a rock. Some creative folders have combined even more subjects, such as several birds in a nest. Use a square of origami paper coloured side up, or for a better effect, two differently coloured or textured sheets folded back to back.

Designed by Dr Martin Wall, UK.

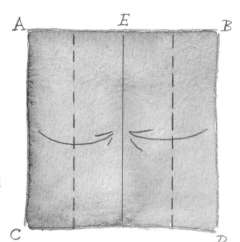

1 Crease and unfold down the centre, then fold the sides to the middle.

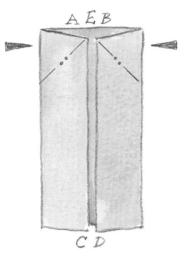

2 Reverse fold the top two corners.

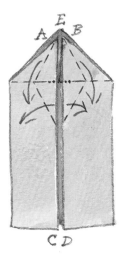 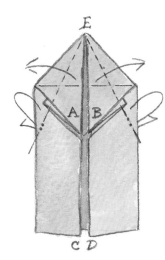 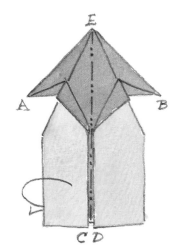 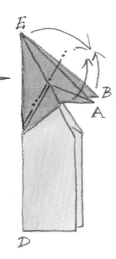

3 Collapse, folding A & B downwards and adding the reverse folds.

4 Fold as shown, allowing A & B to swivel outwards.

5 Mountain fold A behind.

6 Reverse fold E, allowing A & B to pivot upwards to touch E.

 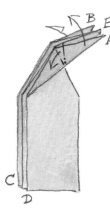  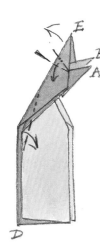 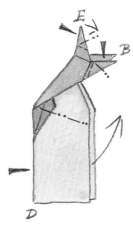

7 Narrow the paper with two reverse folds.

8 Pleat A & B.

9 Turn E inside out, lowering A & B.

10 Crimp the neck upwards. Release paper for the tail. Repeat behind.

11 Crimp the head. Squash the flippers. Reverse fold the rock.

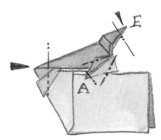  

12 Reverse fold the snout. Round off the flippers. Sink the excess paper inside at the tail.

13 Crimp the rock to make it 3D.

14 The Seal on a Rock complete.

BOWL

Dr Shen is renowned for his geometric and abstract forms which collapse dramatically into shape from an apparently unpromising pattern of pre-creases. In this example, note how the soft, cushion-like base makes an effective contrast to the straight-sided walls. The locking mechanism in Steps 13–14 is also pleasing. Use a square of origami paper, white side up, or paper the same colour both sides.

Designed by Dr Philip Shen, Hong Kong.

1 Crease mountains and valleys as shown.

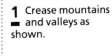
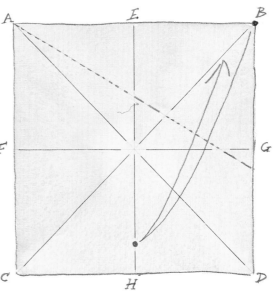

2 Lightly lay corner B onto crease HE, in such a position that if the paper were flattened to make a crease, the crease would run exactly to corner A. However, flatten to make a crease *only* in the two short sections shown. Be precise.

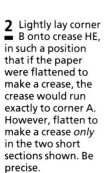

3 Repeat, laying corner C onto crease GF.

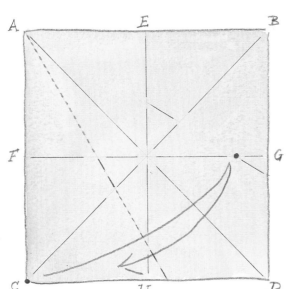
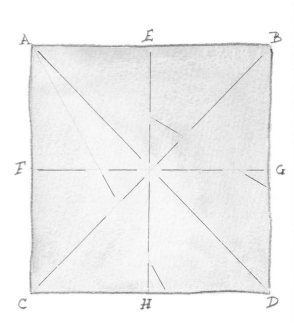

4 Note the crease pattern, both pairs of creases pointing to corner A. Repeat the pattern, so that pairs of creases point to corners B,C, & D.

5 Note the octagon of creases in the centre and the 'V's' at E,F,G, & H. Fold B to point I, but crease only where shown. Similarly, fold C to J. Note that if extended, both creases would meet at corner A.

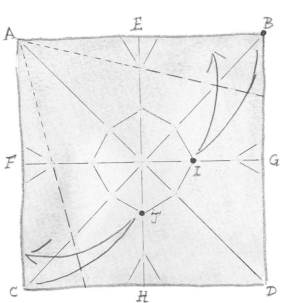
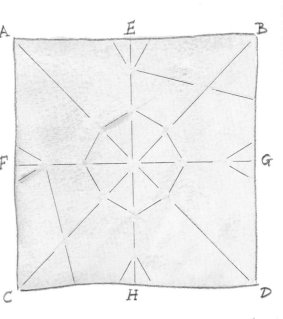

6 This is the crease pattern. Repeat Step 5, creating creases which if extended, would meet at corners B,C, & D.

(Continued . . .)

7 This is the present crease pattern.

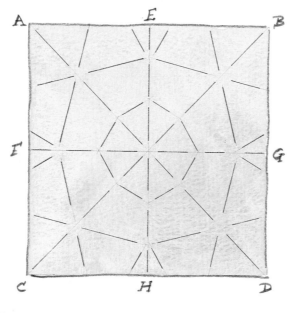

8 Form crease KL to the left of corner A, then repeat with similar creases to the left of each corner, rotating the square 90° each time.

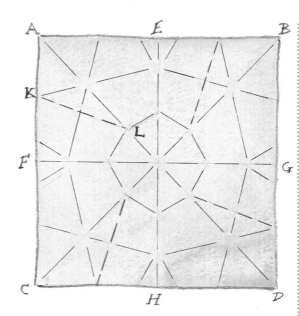

9 Form a pleat along AL & KL, making the paper 3D. Note that L is concave, not convex.

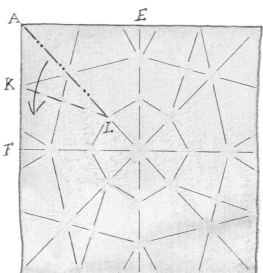

10 Fold A to the right along existing creases. Repeat with B, C & D, folding them also to the right.

11 Collapse all the way round the bowl. Note the pleat at F, repeated at E,G & H.

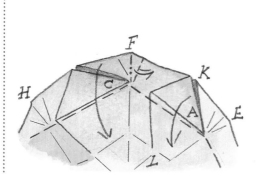

12 This is the bowl at present – a loose, badly-locked and rather lumpy form. Turn it upside down.

13 Form a mountain as shown . . .

14 . . . to create a flat-bottomed bowl standing on four squat, flat triangles. These flat triangles trap the K corners inside their layers, so neatening the inside of the bowl. Turn over.

15 The Bowl complete. Note the soft, cushion-like form of the bottom.

ELEPHANT

This final design in the advanced origami section is appropriately the most difficult. Step 7 contains a fiendish closed sink, which will have even the most experienced folders fumbling a little. The Step 11 half-closed sink is little better. It is puzzling to wonder why a design which looks so little like a real elephant should be so immediately recognizable as one! Use a square of paper, same colour both sides. If using origami paper, the coloured side should be outside at Step 1.

Designed by Paul Jackson.

(Continued . . .)

1 Begin with Step 6 of the Waterbomb project. Fold A across to the right.

2 Fold A & D across to edge EC . . .

3 . . . like this, so that when the crease is made, it is precisely horizontal. Unfold it.

4 Unfold A & D, then swivel B upwards to create the Step 5 shape.

5 Squash, separating F from G.

6 Fold G behind.

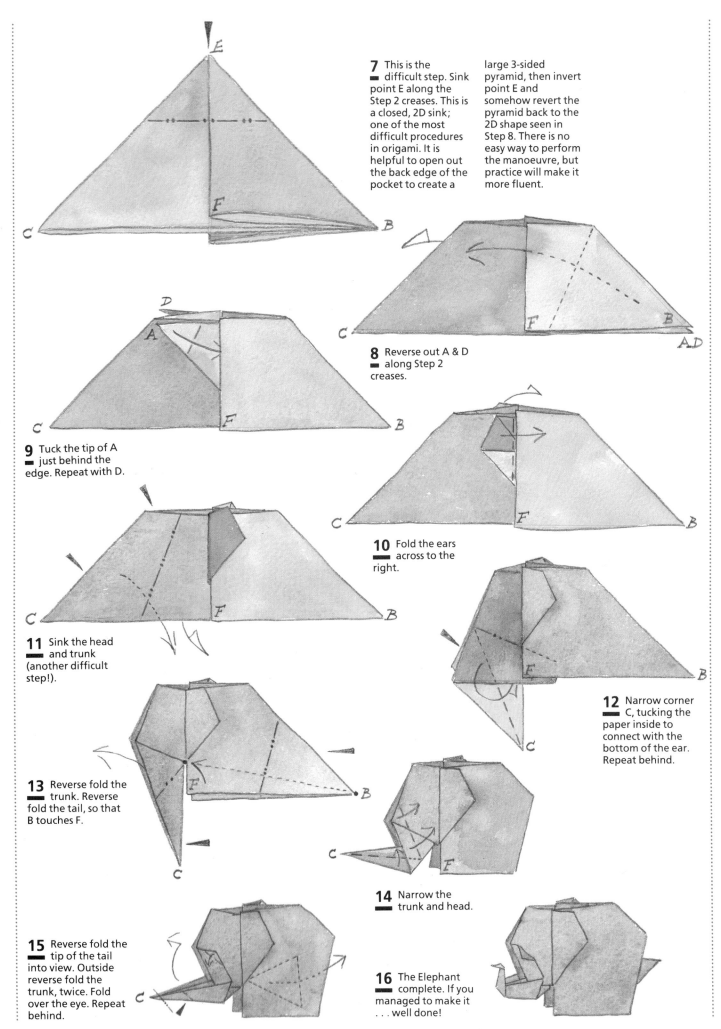

7 This is the difficult step. Sink point E along the Step 2 creases. This is a closed, 2D sink; one of the most difficult procedures in origami. It is helpful to open out the back edge of the pocket to create a large 3-sided pyramid, then invert point E and somehow revert the pyramid back to the 2D shape seen in Step 8. There is no easy way to perform the manoeuvre, but practice will make it more fluent.

8 Reverse out A & D along Step 2 creases.

9 Tuck the tip of A just behind the edge. Repeat with D.

10 Fold the ears across to the right.

11 Sink the head and trunk (another difficult step!).

12 Narrow corner C, tucking the paper inside to connect with the bottom of the ear. Repeat behind.

13 Reverse fold the trunk. Reverse fold the tail, so that B touches F.

14 Narrow the trunk and head.

15 Reverse fold the tip of the tail into view. Outside reverse fold the trunk, twice. Fold over the eye. Repeat behind.

16 The Elephant complete. If you managed to make it . . . well done!

CHOCOLATE BOX

This box is quick and easy to assemble. It needs only a spot of glue and a few tucks. Fill it with chocolates or homemade truffles for the perfect gift.

YOU WILL NEED
Thin coloured card
Craft knife
Glue

1 First, scale up the pattern from the template to the size required and transfer to the piece of card. Cut out using a craft knife, scoring along the back of the creases. Glue the end tab to form the basic box shape.

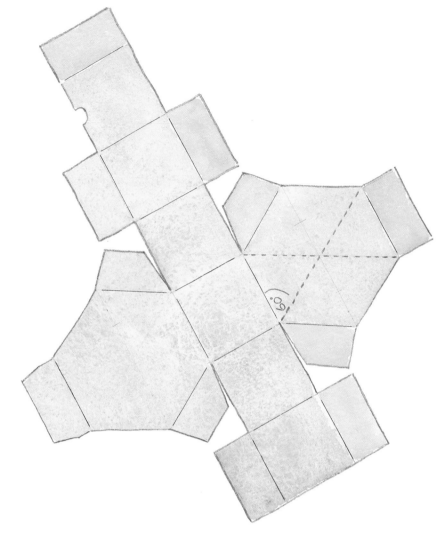

2 Next, interlock the tabs at the base of the box. If the pattern has been carefully cut out, the base will lock strongly without glue. Fill the box with sweets and fold down the lid.

PRACTICAL ENVELOPE

Home-made envelopes can be cheaper and a lot more fun than shop-bought ones. Make a set from a variety of different papers, both plain and patterned. In order to write the address on a patterned paper simply add a little white label.

YOU WILL NEED
Stiff paper
Glue

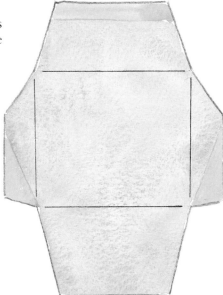

1 Scale up the template to the size required and transfer to the stiff paper. Using a scissor blade, gently score along the back of the creases that are to be folded. Next, fold in the side flaps.

2 Glue the bottom flap to the side flaps to form the envelope. Pop in your letter or card, seal with a dab of glue and send it off!

DECORATIVE
WALLET

Make this tidy wallet out of a favourite colour paper or piece of wrapping paper. You could even design the pattern yourself. Use the wallet to store banknotes, photographs or special letters.

YOU WILL NEED
Stiff paper or *wrapping paper*
Craft knife
Glue

1 Scale up the template to the size required and transfer the pattern onto the paper. Cut around the edges using a craft knife. Fold the sides inwards and glue one long edge to the other.

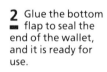

2 Glue the bottom flap to seal the end of the wallet, and it is ready for use.

CURVY-EDGED BOX

This unusual box is almost as pretty in two halves as it is when assembled. To get the maximum effect choose two contrasting or complementary colours for the two halves so that the pattern of the curves stands out.

YOU WILL NEED
Thin card in two different colours
Craft knife
Glue

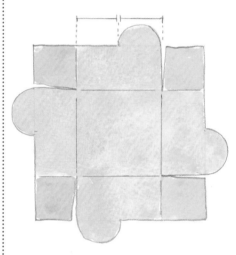

1 Scale up the template to the size required and transfer the pattern twice to a piece of card, once for each half of the box. Cut out the patterns using a craft knife, taking extra care around the curves. Both halves are made in the same way: fold and glue each tab beneath the semi-circles to form the sides.

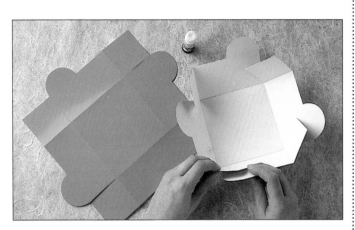

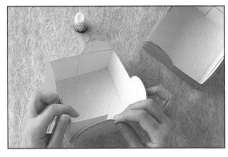

2 Repeat the process with the other half, gluing each side firmly.

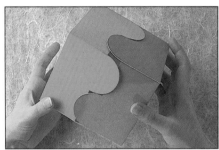

3 To assemble the box, interlock the two halves, making sure each semi-circle overlaps on the outside of the box.

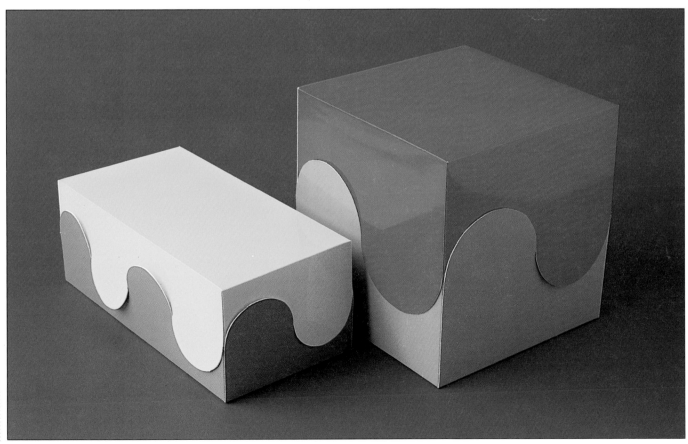

CONCENTRIC TWIST

Hang this impressive paper sculpture in a window; if it is made from metallic-coated card it will catch the light as it moves gently in the air currents.

YOU WILL NEED
Thin coloured card
Craft knife

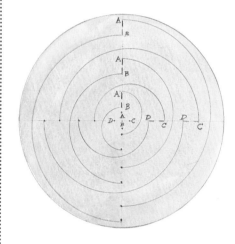

1 Scale up the template to the required size and transfer to coloured card. Cut the slits using a craft knife. Gently twist the central circle away from its frame.

2 Starting at the rim, form the first twist again by gently turning the central section at an angle of 90 degrees to the outer ring.

3 Continue to form the twists by turning each ring at the same angle, moving progressively towards the centre, until the twist-out is complete.

LIDDED BOX

This box can be used to keep things safe – or to conceal a surprise. Make several in a variety of colours to form a set or give one to each of your friends.

YOU WILL NEED
Thin coloured card
Craft knife
Glue

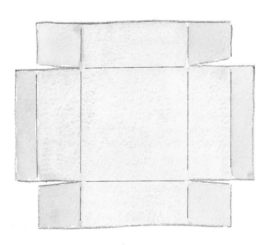

1 The box and its lid are made in the same way. Scale up the template to the size required and transfer the pattern to thin coloured card. Carefully cut out the pieces using a craft knife. Fold in the side tabs to form the upright sides.

2 Next, assemble the box by applying glue to the central tabs and folding them over the sides, fixing down firmly. Repeat this process to make the lid, and slide it over the base to complete the box.

INDEX